Move It.
Lose It.
Live Healthy.

The Simple Truth About Achieving & Maintaining a Healthy Body Weight

Thomas B. Gilliam, Ph.D. and Jane Neill, R.D., L.D.

ISBN-13: 978-0-9762703-5-5
ISBN-10: 0-9762703-5-8
Library of Congress Control Number: 2007940083

Publisher:
T. Gilliam & Associates, LLC
1696 Georgetown Road, Unit B
Hudson, OH 44236
To order multiple copies of this publication, go to:
www.moveitloseitlivehealthy.com

Cover Design: Jon C. Lund
Designs and Illustrations: Susan Woodward

The information contained in this book is not intended to represent
a medical diagnosis, treatment, or medical advice in any way, as it is
general information and cannot be relied on without consultation with
your physician. It is not intended nor is it implied to be a substitute for
professional medical advice. In fact, taking full advantage of this program
will require that you consult with your physician or a physician willing to
work with you. As medical information and your health can change
rapidly, we strongly encourage you to discuss all health matters and
concerns with your physician before beginning new diagnostic or
treatment strategies.

The people, incidents and dialogue discussed in this book are borrowed
from the authors' collective experience, but do not represent actual people
or events. Any resemblance to actual persons, living or dead, is entirely
coincidental.

Dedication

To a healthier and more productive person.

Acknowledgments

Move It. Lose It. Live Healthy.: The Simple Truth About Achieving & Maintaining a Healthy Body Weight is the product of many ideas and experiences that evolved over a 20-year period. The inspiration for this book came from many of our friends, business associates and family members who would ask common sense questions about how to achieve a healthy lifestyle. To all of you, we thank you for taking the time to ask us those questions.

We are grateful to Dick Schneider for his editorial comments. Dick is the former editor-in-chief of *Hydraulics and Pneumatics,* published by Penton Publishing.

A special thanks to Susan Woodward of S.E. Woodward Designs, Jon C. Lund of Jon C. Lund Illustration and David Mitchell for their creative design and artwork.

Our sincerest thanks to Elizabeth Gilliam, Kathleen Gilliam Knox and Richard Hoffman for their editorial comments and for the creation of many of the children's stories.

We are deeply grateful to our families for their support while writing this book.

Foreword

Obesity has no boundaries. It is impacting people of all ages around the world. Young, old, men and women are all experiencing very serious levels of obesity. And now America's children have reached a level of obesity that is epidemic.

The impact obesity is having on our society is alarming. It impacts the health of our society, our ability to be productive and our ability to compete. The economic future of our society does not look very bright unless we begin to actively take control of the factors that contribute to obesity. Two critical factors, which we can control, are physical activity and nutrition.

Unfortunately, marketers are taking advantage of the obesity epidemic by offering quick fixes. These don't work to your benefit in the long-term.

The purpose of this book is to teach adults, parents and children how to become more physically active and to eat more nutritiously. The book is divided into three sections. The first two sections focus on physical activity and proper nutrition for the adult population, and the third section is directed to families with children.

This book focuses on achieving a healthy body weight. For some individuals, their body weight may be near normal now but as they grow older they may be concerned about how to keep that normal body weight and not add any weight. This book describes how to accomplish that goal.

For some individuals, their body weight might be too much now and perhaps a few additional pounds are being added each year. As a result, over the next ten years, a substantial weight gain will take place that is not healthy. This book discusses how to gradually take off the weight that has been gained over the years and how to prevent further gain.

The information in this book is not a substitute for medical advice or treatment. The book provides sound, healthful information to help readers to better understand healthy exercise and nutritional habits. This information should help readers make better healthy lifestyle choices to improve their health. Should you have any questions about your health, consult your physician or healthcare provider.

Move It. Lose It. Live Healthy.
The Simple Truth About Achieving & Maintaining a Healthy Body Weight

This book is for adults and families with children!

Table of Contents

Section Three – The Heart "E" Heart Approach
to a Healthy Lifestyle for Children
and Their Parents

Section One

An Adult Guide to a More Physically Active Lifestyle

A Common Sense Approach

Chapter 1:
Introduction

Obesity and Type II diabetes, which are both pre-ventable, have reached epidemic stages for individu-als of all ages because of a lack of physical activity and poor nutritional habits!

Today, more than ever, we have the resources and ability to take control of our health. Experience tells us that most people are very interested in taking good care of their health. Experience also tells us that most people need some direction and information that makes sense, with goals that arc achievable. Our children need the most direction but many parents acknowledge that they don't know how to get their children to live a healthy lifestyle.

For many years now, our society has become increasingly unfit and over-weight, due to lack of physical activity and poor nutritional habits. As a result, obesity and diabetes have reached the epidemic state for both adults and children. What makes this even more horrific is that more of our children will be exposed to a lifetime of obesity and diabetes than any other generation of children in the history of our country. The impact of this on their health as they become adults will result in a very serious medical and economic burden to our society.

Obesity is an epidemic in the United States. Most research shows that at least 60 percent of the American population is either overweight or obese. Some studies put the figure as high as 74 percent. It is a grave concern to health experts because it is linked with so many other problems and illnesses such as heart disease, diabetes, high blood pressure (hypertension), high triglycerides, high cholesterol (especially the unhealthy cholesterol called low density lipoprotein), osteoarthritis, certain forms of cancer and many other health disorders. In fact, because of this obesity problem, diabetes is now an epidemic in the United States.

Why has obesity reached the epidemic level?

- Some experts blame this dilemma on what our health standards were some 15 years ago. You may recall that most of the health standards in the 1970s and '80s were based on normative standards, or "norms," instead of what was healthy. And most of these norms had age built into them. The norm for systolic blood pressure was 100 plus your age. Cholesterol was 200 plus your age. Body weight tables were based on height and age. The experts back then were saying it was okay to have higher systolic blood pressure or higher cholesterol or to gain weight as you grow older. Today, the norms are based on what is needed to keep us healthy. Age is no longer a factor.

- Another possible explanation is the incredible growth of the fast food industry and the larger (super-sized) portions of food consumed.

- Others say it is because we have become so dependent on machines doing our work that we don't have enough physical activity in our daily lives.

- And some say our children watch way too much TV and spend too much time playing video games instead of being physically active.

No matter what the reason or who or what is to blame, we have a very serious health problem in the United States. This will have a devastating long-term effect on our ability to work and perform in a global economy.

Experience Tells Us We Have a Problem!

As a tenured faculty member at the University of Michigan, I was involved with funded research to study cardiovascular risk factors in children in the 1970s. Jane Neill, a registered dietitian at the University of Michigan, was involved with this same research. Our work clearly showed that children in the 1970s were at risk for cardiovascular disease primarily because of a lack of intense vigorous physical activity. Although poor nutrition was a factor, it was less of a threat. Also, the percentage of children at risk for cardiovascular disease (and related diseases such as obesity) was much lower than it is today.

The authors also discovered that children could not be forced to become more physically active or eat more nutritiously. But when an educational program was introduced to teach primary grade children why they should become more physically active and eat nutritiously, they did. So the authors knew then that if

the right education program were put forth, children would make the appropriate lifestyle behavior changes.

Perhaps if more had been done in the 1970s for our children, we would not have such a serious obesity problem now in the 21st century.

Since 1980, I have been providing physical capability strength testing programs in industry to match the physical capability of the worker to the physical demands of the job. My testing has shown the number of individuals who can't be placed into physically demanding jobs is much higher today than in the 1980s. The primary reasons are obesity and poor physical fitness. Research clearly shows a link between obesity and the lack of ability to perform physically demanding work.

Obesity is also the cause for a rise in workplace disability rates for individuals in the age range of 30 to 49 years. These individuals, who should be in their prime, are the ones whom industry is very dependent upon to fill critical, productive jobs.

What does this data mean for industry and for the people needed to sustain our economy and global competition?

The news is not good! Individuals whom industry normally counts on to perform physically demanding jobs are becoming more and more unhealthy and unfit. These individuals are now costing companies more money in terms of injuries, illnesses and disability. This impacts every company across all industries because at least 60 percent of the workforce is either overweight or obese. The pool of healthy workers available to perform physically demanding jobs is rapidly shrinking. Companies are hiring individuals today who will be costing them much more money in direct costs related to injury and illness as well as indirect costs related to loss of productivity and increases in training costs, as more replacements will be needed to cover those individuals on disability!

This means the cost of goods that we purchase can do only one thing and that is to go up! Now this impacts all of us!

What is even more serious is that the ability of a company to compete globally is dramatically reduced because of the obesity epidemic. Since obesity is not going away and because the children in America also have an obesity epidemic, companies will continue to hire more unfit and unhealthy individuals for many years to come!

Why should you care? Because you and other workers want better benefits and higher wages. It is difficult for companies to improve benefits and provide higher wages when so much more of the company's money is going to support illnesses that could be prevented. The average cost of a disability claim caused by obesity for a worker in 2004 was $51,000 per year. With over 60 percent of the workforce either overweight or obese, the number of these claims and costs of these claims can only go up. This means less money is available to improve benefits and wages.

What can you do? Begin to put into place some very simple practices—discussed in this book—designed to help you maintain a healthy body weight. This is better for your personal health and for the economic health of your employer.

The irony of the obesity problem is that for the most part we have made it easier to occur. We have done a great job engineering the physical part out of most jobs (at home and at work). We have taken play away from our children so that they no longer expend enough calories on a daily basis to offset the number of calories they consume from the food they eat. While we might overindulge in terms of food we eat, the lack of physical activity poses a more serious problem. *While obesity is preventable, we as a society seem to be working against its prevention.*

Most research shows that Americans are consuming more calories and expending even fewer calories on a daily basis than we did ten years ago.

Today your health needs to be taken very seriously. We are bombarded with diets of all kinds, food supplements that are sup-

posed to make us look good and feel 30 years younger, gadgets to get rid of all of our fat and so on. For the most part, these quick programs and gadgets are money makers for those who sell them, but they do not contribute anything to your health and well-being in the long run. The manufacturers and developers of these substandard health fixes know that many consumers will try anything that is quick and involves a minimum of effort.

Almost everything you need to do to enhance your health can be done with a common sense approach, using a few items that you already have in your home.

Losing weight and becoming more physically fit takes time and it must be kept simple. Overloading an individual with too many things to keep track of in terms of what to eat and what activities to do becomes a burden, and soon the program fails.

The authors of this book strongly believe that understanding why and how to exercise and to eat more nutritiously is critical before any changes can be made to your lifestyle.

Knowledge works! People choose questionable quick fixes because they don't understand how their bodies function or the role of exercise and good nutrition. If they did understand, they would no longer rely on the quick fix method. This book provides the reasons why exercise is important and how to do it correctly. The same is true for nutrition. Once you have a good foundation and understanding of these very important and critical components to preventing obesity and related diseases, you will make positive changes in your lifestyle that will lead to long-term benefits. If you are looking for a quick fix to lose weight or become more physically active, this book is not for you.

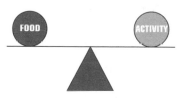

Chapter 2:
We Must Walk Before We Run!

Based on current research, the cause of the obesity epidemic today is a combination of our eating habits and lack of physical activity. Most research shows that Americans are consuming more calories and expending even fewer calories on a daily basis than we did ten years ago.

It is our opinion that there is great confusion about how much physical activity we really need and what is the best way to maintain a healthy body weight.

Controlling Your Body Weight

▸ What is body weight?

▸ How do you lose weight?

▸ Why do you gain weight?

▸ How can you keep your weight the same?

▸ Does my body weight change with age?

There are very simple answers to these questions. Once you learn the answers, you will realize that losing weight by using one of the fad diets on the market today is not a smart approach to a healthy lifestyle and a healthy body weight. The only time a special diet should be considered is when someone has a disease such as diabetes, heart disease or something similar, where controlling the kinds of food eaten is critical.

What Is Body Weight?

Your weight is controlled by calories! It is that simple. The food consumed is measured in calories, which can also be referred to as energy intake. All of your body's activities, from your heart beating to riding a bike, can be measured in calories, too. This is your energy output or expenditure. Your energy output is divided into two components – energy for routine daily activities and energy for physical activity or exercise such as riding a bike, walking or playing a sport.

Your daily metabolic rate is the amount of energy needed to sustain life and for routine daily activities.   It takes energy for your heart to beat, lungs to breathe, kidneys to work, to digest food, to eat, to sleep, to get dressed, to clean the house, do the dishes, work and so on.

Essentially these two items – calories consumed and calories used or expended – make up the equation that controls your body weight.

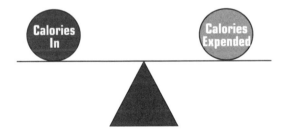

How Do You Lose Weight?

If the number of calories that you consume each day is less than the number of calories expended, you will lose weight over time. Again, it is that simple.

If Amount of Calories Consumed Is Less Than Amount of Calories Expended,

You Lose Weight!

To lose a pound of fat, you have to expend 3,500 calories more than you consume. This difference can be accomplished by:

▶ Consuming fewer calories each day

▶ Expending more calories each day

▶ Or a combination of both

Any effort to lose weight should be done over an extended period of time such as one year.

Just a few minor changes in reducing your calories consumed or increasing the calories expended can result in a 10-20 pound weight loss over 12 months. For example, let's say you consume two 12-ounce soft drinks a day. The average number of calories in a soft drink is 140. Not a lot by itself. But what would happen if you eliminated one soft drink a day from your eating habits for an entire year and changed nothing else? (You could replace the soft drink with a 12-ounce glass of water – another positive lifestyle change.) The final result would be that you eliminated 51,100 (365 days times 140) calories from your diet for the entire year. Since one pound of fat is equal to 3,500 calories, this could result in about a 15-pound weight loss for the entire year (51,100 divided by 3,500).

Besides eliminating one soft drink a day, let us say that you also added 15 minutes of physical activity every day to your daily routine for the entire year. This 15-minute activity would result in about 91 hours of more physical activity each year. This could result in roughly another five to ten pounds of weight loss, depending on your current body weight.

Sometimes a question is raised about the kinds of food consumed.

▶ Can I lose weight faster by choosing certain kinds of foods over other kinds of foods?

  • Different kinds of foods will impact your health but not necessarily your weight loss.

  • Remember, a calorie is a calorie; it does not matter if it comes from a cookie or from a peach. A peach is healthier than a cookie, though.

None of the diets on the market today are necessary for weight loss. It all boils down to calories – if you control the calories consumed relative to the calories expended, you can control your body weight.

Think of your body weight as a teeter-totter. On one end of the teeter-totter is food consumed each day (calories taken in) and on the other end are your daily physical activities (calories expended). If both of these items are in balance or equal, the teeter-totter is level – it does not tip one way or the other – you don't gain weight or lose weight.

But if the calories taken in are greater than the caloric output, the teeter-totter tips to the side that adds body weight. In contrast, if the amount of energy expended is greater than the calories consumed, the teeter-totter tips to the other side and body weight is lost.

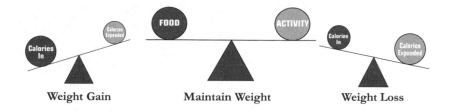

Weight Gain   Maintain Weight   Weight Loss

The Body Likes to Be in Balance

Although controlling your body weight does seem simple, the body makes it much more difficult. Located in the brain is a nerve center that acts to control your body weight by controlling your hunger. The body has a "set point" controlled by this nerve center that keeps our body weight fairly constant – even though your weight can be too much, too little or just right. The set point doesn't like change, especially rapid change, because the body likes to remain in balance or "homeostasis." The set point can be altered but only through small, gradual changes. Small changes help maintain a sense of "homeostasis" or balance, which the body will accept.

That is one reason why fad diets, quick fixes or radical diets don't work for the long-term. Oh yes, you may lose weight quickly but after the diet ends, the weight is put back on and most times more than what was lost during the diet. Why?

- Because the "set point" for your body weight was not altered when you took the weight off too fast, and

- The body will fight rapid change to keep its "homeostasis."

That is why to lose weight, you need to do it slowly, over time. This allows the "set point" to be adjusted downward, slowly, so your weight loss will be permanent. By doing it slowly, the body can adjust to this gradual change more easily and stay in balance.

How Can I Gain Weight? How Can I Keep My Body Weight the Same?

The answer to these questions is similar to the weight loss question. To gain weight, you should consume more calories each day than you expend. Again, keep in mind that just small changes in either the food you consume or your daily physical activities can alter the equation. Any weight gain should be done slowly just like weight loss. Adding weight slowly, tied into a physical activity program such as weightlifting, will mean the weight added will be mostly muscle and not fat.

To maintain your body weight, you should consume the same number of calories each day as you expend.

Does My Body Weight Change with My Age?

It wasn't too many years ago that the "norms" for body weight showed that as you got older, your body weight should increase. But now we know that there are healthy limits for body weight instead of "norms" and that your body weight should not increase just because your age increases.

One item that does impact your body weight as you grow older is your "resting metabolic rate" (RMR). The RMR is the amount of energy needed to sustain your daily activities - the heart to beat, lungs to breathe, working, eating, driving a car and

so on. RMR tends to slow down as you age. This means you require fewer calories to sustain your daily activities. This also happens because the body tends to lose muscle as it gets older and it gains more fat. Fat burns fewer calories than muscle, which means your RMR will slow down as you get older. This normally does not have any significant impact on body weight until after the age of 50 when the RMR slows down the most. As a result, it is not uncommon for your body weight to increase after the age of 50 with no changes to your eating habits or physical activity habits. So what daily adjustments should you make to your lifestyle after the age of 50?

- consume slightly *fewer* calories, or
- increase your physical activity level, or
- keep as much muscle as possible through a strength training program or
- all of the above!

These adjustments will offset the slow down in your RMR. This should keep your weight from increasing as you enter those wonderful "golden years."

Certain physical activities such as strength training or lifting weights will help keep the RMR at a decent level as you age. Lifting weights will increase protein (muscle) metabolism, which delays the slow down of the RMR. This is something to keep in mind as you begin to select physical activities for your healthy lifestyle from the following chapters.

Unfortunately, many young adults (under the age of 50) have gained just a little weight each year (three or four pounds). On a yearly basis, that doesn't seem like much, but when this happens over ten years, the weight gain is too much (now 30 or 40 pounds). The weight gain probably happened by consuming just a few more calories each day than what were expended (either you were eating too much or you became less physically active). Now you want to take it off.

Just remember it took you ten years to gain the weight so don't expect to lose it in just weeks. This is another reason why the authors' recommended approach to losing weight is to do it slowly over time – not to seek a quick fix.

How Much Physical Activity Do You Really Need?

Twenty years ago, the exercise experts were saying that you needed one hour of aerobic exercise three times a week! No consideration was given to your daily activities such as working, cleaning, cutting grass and so on.

Today, it is important to include as much physical activity in your daily routine as possible. The American College of Sports Medicine and the American Heart Association now encourage all individuals to participate in at least 30 minutes of moderate physical activity five days per week in addition to your normal daily activities to achieve good health. If weight loss is your goal, it is recommended that you add 30 minutes of lighter physical activity, such as a leisurely walk, each day. Moderate physical activities can include chores such as vacuuming, cutting the lawn (walking), and gardening and physical activities such as brisk walking, swimming, hiking, biking (greater than 10 mph), and some team sports such as basketball and soccer. Individual sports such as singles tennis, racquetball, and golf (walking) are good moderate activities.

Some individuals need a regimen of knowing that they are doing a specific amount of exercise each time they work out. In that case, a fitness center works best because you can track your time and distance on a machine like a treadmill. Or it may involve swimming laps for a certain amount of time or completing a certain number of laps.

Sometimes it is possible to do the same thing at home by mapping out a neighborhood walking, jogging, rollerblading or

cycling course. If you know the distance, then you can track your cumulative distances and time involved with the physical activity. If possible, select alternative routes so you can vary the course from time to time to keep it interesting. One advantage of setting up a course at home is that you can involve the entire family on walks or on bicycle rides. Sometimes a family member will walk while a child rides a bike or rollerblades. You don't all have to be doing the same thing – the important thing is that you are all becoming physically active.

How Important Are Daily Activities?

Besides the exercise regimen you do on a daily basis, routine daily physical activities are also very important. Some occupations are very physically demanding, such as construction workers, carpenters, laborers or firefighters. These kinds of jobs generally provide adequate physical activity to maintain a healthy lifestyle so that doing other physical activity or exercise routines when arriving home may not be necessary. Just remember not to overeat while on the job or at home.

But what about jobs that are not physically demanding? If you are not involved in a physically demanding job, it is important to add as much physical activity to your daily routine as possible.

Taking the stairs while at work instead of taking the elevators, parking farther from the building so you need to walk, taking walking breaks instead of coffee breaks (instead of consuming calories in snacks, you are expending calories!) – all can help you achieve a healthier lifestyle.

Many parking structures are good places to walk while at work (caution – don't walk alone; find a buddy to walk with).

Parking structures are protected from inclement weather such as rain and snow. However, parking structures can be dangerous if the ventilation is not adequate, especially those underground – so check it out first.

Sometimes it is possible to join a fitness center near your place of employment, or your employer may have a fitness center on-site or offer a fitness membership as a health benefit. In these cases, it is possible to get your exercise routine in before you get home.

There are many ways to increase your physical activity while at home. Gardening, cutting grass (walking behind the mower), laundry, vacuuming and scrubbing floors are all ways to involve the entire family and increase their level of physical  activity at the same time. Remember to involve your children in the household chores. This teaches the children responsibility and it also enhances their self-esteem.

 If you must watch TV, use the commercials as an excuse to get up and move around. Avoiding commercials could be a healthy lifestyle move – at least you won't be tempted with all kinds of foods, drinks and pills to consume.

Those of you who like to shop can use your shopping experience as a physical activity. By arriving at the mall or shopping center early, you can walk around for 15 to 20 min-  utes before beginning to shop. Use the time to plan your shopping spree or to get ideas as you walk past store fronts. Some experts suggest parking farther from the stores so you need to walk further to start shopping. But if you do, you must be careful as to where you park – make sure it is safe! Some malls open early, especially in areas where the weather is not always cooperative, so you can come in and use the mall as a walking course.

Remember what was said at the beginning of this section. The most important consideration is the accumulation of physical activity on a daily basis, including moderate activities. If you don't have the time to exercise for a continuous hour, that is okay. For example, walking 15 to 20 minutes in the morning and riding your bike for 30 minutes in the evening in addition to whatever activity you do while at work will take care of your daily physical activity requirement. There are many ways to achieve that one hour of daily physical activity – you just need to be a little creative.

Building Muscle Is Good for Weight Loss

Another important piece of the physical activity puzzle needs to be mentioned. Most of the emphasis over the years has been on aerobic activities. These are activities that are continuous and normally last 30 minutes or more, such as walking, jogging, swimming, biking and so on.

But building muscle strength or preventing its loss is just as important. Keeping your muscles strong helps to protect your joints and to prevent diseases such as osteoporosis in later years. Also, remember what was said when discussing resting metabolic rate (RMR). Weightlifting will increase muscle (protein) metabolism, which tends to keep your RMR elevated as you age. This could help prevent adding weight to your body as you grow older. But don't let the words weightlifting frighten you. There are many strength building activities that can be done right in your own home. (See Chapter 4, page 56 for more information).

Counting Calories Does Work

Finally, you have now read about both sides of the body weight equation. Food represents the calories consumed and physical activity represents calories expended. If you keep the calories consumed in balance with the calories expended, you won't gain weight. If you con-  sume fewer calories than what you expend, you will lose weight – it is just that simple.

Some of you may be wondering why the title of this chapter is "We Must Walk Before We Run!" Our experience is that most individuals try to make too many changes to their lifestyle at one time – they start out running. When this happens, you are  doomed. You must start simply and eventually many positive healthy lifestyle habits will become just that – habits. Healthy choices will become routine in your daily life. That is when you suc- ceed in achieving a healthy body weight.

Chapter 3:
Let's Get Moving!

Before you begin any kind of physical activity or exercise program, you should make sure that medically you can participate in the physical activity. If you have any condition that would prevent you from exercising or limit your ability to perform exercises, you should always obtain clearance from your doctor before beginning. It is not a bad idea to let your doctor know that you are participating in new healthy lifestyle changes that involve physical activity and nutritional habits. Your doctor would be pleased to know that information!

Whenever you participate in a physical activity, safety should be your primary concern during the activity. Too many times, individuals cause more harm to their bodies than good because they try to do too much too quickly. In Chapter 2, we said that you should walk before you run. That is true when beginning your physical activity program as well.

Getting Started!

If it has been three months or more since you participated in a physical activity program and during this period of time your lifestyle has been mostly sedentary (very inactive), then you want to make sure you start slowly. Further, it is recommended that you consult with your physician before you begin. If you do too much too quickly, you can cause injury to your body. You then may become discouraged and quit. No one wins under this scenario!

When starting an exercise program, the key word is *gradual*. Everything involved in your physical activity program should be done *gradually*. The length of time of your exercise program should increase *gradually*. Changes to your exercise routine should be done *gradually*. The speed (intensity) at which you do the exercise should increase *gradually*.

It takes time to increase your level of physical fitness. The longer it has been since you last regularly exercised, the longer it will take you to realize the benefits of your new exercise program. Again, this concept goes back to what was said in Chapter 1 – this book is not meant to be a quick fix but instead to bring about permanent changes in your lifestyle habits that will be very beneficial to you and your family.

There are several key components to any exercise program that apply to any kind of physical activity – even to your occupation if you have a physically demanding job or to a physically demanding chore at home such as shoveling snow.

Key Components to Getting Started

The key components are the warm-up, the actual activity and the cool-down.

- The warm-up prepares your body for the actual physical activity. It usually lasts several minutes and consists of slow-moving routines that involve stretching and other movements to slowly increase the heart rate and increase blood flow to the arms and legs.

- The actual activity should last from 15 minutes to an hour. Remember, it is the accumulative effect that is important, so you may exercise two or three times during the day, which will add up to one hour.

- The cool-down allows the heart to slow down gradually, return to its pre-exercise level and for the muscles to be stretched again. The cool-down phase normally lasts several minutes. Physical activity generates heat. Body temperature will increase because of the exercise, which is normal. Taking time after you exercise to cool down actually starts the cooling effect on your body. How long and how fast you exercised will determine how long the cool-down will take. In some instances, it may take several hours. For example, after you stop exercising and even after you take a shower, you might continue to perspire for a period of time, especially in a warm environment. Perspiring helps to cool the body.

Stretching exercises will be discussed in detail in Chapter 4. A proper warm-up and cool-down will help prevent muscle soreness, especially when you are just beginning your exercise routine.

Safety Concerns!

Today there are all kinds of exercises that require safety

 gear. Riding a bicycle is a very good exercise and can involve the entire family. But make sure you wear a helmet and that your child wears one too! (Helmets should also be worn when riding a

motorized scooter.) Ideally, purchase your helmet from a bicycle shop and ask for assistance in fitting the helmet to your head. A helmet that is not fitted properly will offer very little protection if you fall. Also, most helmets provide maximum protection for up to two or three years and then the helmet's material becomes brittle. At this point, the helmet's protective capability is limited. It is suggested at this time you purchase a new helmet. If you are riding a bike in the street, abide by all highway traffic rules. Ride single file with the flow of traffic. *Do not ride against the flow of traffic.*   (For additional information on bike safety see the month of July, Chapter 14).

Skateboarding, rollerblading and similar kinds of activities also require protective gear besides a helmet. Wrist guards and elbow and knee pads offer additional protection and are strongly recommended.

Swimming is an excellent exercise. Swimming in a pool that has a lifeguard is the safest way to swim. If no lifeguard is present, then always swim with someone else. This is especially important when swimming in a lake or a pond. Never swim by yourself. Also, to be safe, allow at least 30 minutes from the time you ate to when you begin to swim. This allows some time for your food to digest, which requires diverting blood from your arms and legs to the stomach area. When swimming, the blood is diverted back to the arms and legs and away from the stomach, which could cause cramping.

The place you exercise and the time of day you exercise is also a safety concern. If you are walking, jogging or biking, always be aware of your surroundings. Again, try to exercise with a buddy. If you exercise in the evening or early morning when it is dark, make sure you select a lighted course and one that is well traveled by others. Wear a reflective vest so car lights can pick up your image before the car is upon you.

Another safety recommendation is to avoid doing too much. Many people think the more exercise done (if one hour is good, then two hours must be twice as good) and the faster it is done, the quicker their bodies will become physically fit. It doesn't happen that way. That approach to a physical activity program will result in injury to the body. The body is a machine and like any other machine it can be broken. But if you take care of the machine and do not abuse it, the machine will last for a long time. The body is no different. If you abuse it with too much exercise, it will break down. It might not break down immediately, but

it could several years later when you least expect it. Remember, you should do everything *gradually*.

Another very big safety concern that often is overlooked is the use of a sauna, hot tub and/or steam room. Since these items tend to bring relaxation and pleasure, most people don't pay much attention to the potential health problems associated with these activities. Any individual with a heart, cardiovascular or blood pressure problem should avoid these kinds of treatments. This is absolutely critical immediately following a workout (when most people often use them). It is also strongly recommended that children not be allowed to use these treatments mainly because of increased susceptibility to dehydration.

Finally, these safety concerns don't apply only to adults. Take the time to discuss these safety concerns with your child. Set a good example when exercising by using the appropriate protective gear and practice good safety habits. Your child will follow and learn from your example.

What Is Meant by Gradual?

There are a couple of key components to the actual physical activity or exercise you perform.

- The <u>duration</u> of the physical activity is one component. Do you start with 15, 20 or 60 minutes? If you are just beginning a program, starting with 15 or 20 minutes of exercise makes good sense. You can <u>gradually</u> increase the time to 30 minutes or longer, up to one hour. It may take several months before you can exercise continuously for one hour, if that is one of your goals. Your current level of physical fitness will determine how long it will take before you are able to exercise continuously for one hour.

- The <u>speed</u> or <u>intensity</u> in which you exercise is another component. Walking is a good example to use when explaining speed or intensity. Most walkers know the pace they walk, such as a 20-minute mile. This means it takes 20 minutes to walk one mile. If you walk faster (increase the speed or intensity of the walk), then you will decrease the amount of time it takes to walk one mile. The faster you exercise the more intense the exercise becomes and the faster the heart will beat. The faster you ride your bike, walk, run, jog, swim, rollerblade, skateboard or any similar kind of activity, the more intense the exercise. This is also true when doing chores – the faster you vacuum, cut the grass or work in the garden, the more intense the exercise. If you are first beginning to exercise and you go too fast, reaching a <u>duration</u> goal will become more difficult.

■ Another component is <u>frequency</u>. The American College of Sports Medicine and the American Heart Association recommend 30 minutes of moderate physical activity at least five days a week.

Achieving a Good Balance Between Duration and Intensity!

How do you balance duration of exercise with speed or intensity? Is one more important than the other? The answer depends on what you are trying to achieve.

For someone just beginning to exercise, duration is the more important component. As you become more physically fit, you may want to begin to gradually increase the intensity of the exercise. Let's see how this can be accomplished.

Walking is a very good exercise for starters. If you walk for 15 minutes and are not too tired following the walk, then the next time you walk, increase the duration. You may want to increase the time by three-minute intervals. After you become comfortable with the new duration (this may take several weeks or longer), add another three-minute interval to your walk. Eventually, over many weeks, you will have increased the duration of your walk to 30 minutes.

At that time, you can continue to add three-minute intervals. Or, you can begin to adjust the speed at which you walk. Or, you can do both. Don't be surprised if when you first increase the speed or pace of your walk, the duration of your walk decreases by several minutes. Gradually, keeping with your new pace, you will increase your duration to what it was before you increased the speed or pace.

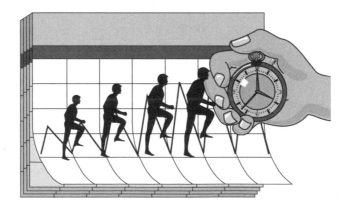

When you begin to plan your exercise program, think in terms of stages instead of planning by the week or month. Once you achieve the objectives for one stage, you move to the next stage. A stage may last one week or one month depending on your level of fitness. The table below shows how duration can increase with each stage, and once an objective of 30 minutes is reached, the intensity can change. As you achieve the objective of the stage, then move to the next one. The objective for some stages may take only a week while others may take longer. Note by stage six, the 30-minute walk objective is achieved so stage seven involves increasing the intensity/pace by increasing the pace of your walk from 3 MPH to 3.2 MPH.

Stage	Duration – Minutes	Intensity/Pace
One	15	20 Minute Mile/3 MPH
Two	18	20 Minute Mile/3 MPH
Three	21	20 Minute Mile/3 MPH
Four	24	20 Minute Mile/3 MPH
Five	27	20 Minute Mile/3 MPH
Six	30	20 Minute Mile/3 MPH
Seven	30	19 Minute Mile/3.2 MPH
Eight	30	18 Minute Mile/3.4 MPH

Changing the duration and speed of exercise applies to many kinds of exercise such as riding a bike, jogging, swimming, rollerblading and so on. Keep in mind that the changes made to the duration and/or speed should be small or gradual changes. Rapid changes or unmanageable increases in duration and/or intensity will cause discomfort and may cause injury.

Once you begin to get into the habit of your exercise routine, you may want to look for alternative exercises. For example, walk one day and ride a bike or swim another day. But keep in mind when you first change from one kind of exercise to another, you might feel some muscle soreness for several days after the initial change. The reason for this is your muscles are being used differently and they need to adjust to the new routine. You can also add new routes to your exercise routine or visit a park to walk or ride a bike on a different course of travel. You can even make a change to your exercise routine by adding hills to your walk, run or bike ride.

The important thing to remember is not the distance you cover but instead the length of time (duration) and speed of the exercise. Also, your goal with the exercise or physical activity program is to increase the number of calories expended from what you are currently expending.

Use Your Calendar!

Each time you complete your exercise for the day, write it down in your calendar for that particular day. Keep track of the duration, kind of exercise performed

(walk, bike and so on) and speed or pace if you know it. Writing it down also adds to your sense of accomplishment on a weekly, monthly and yearly basis. You will be amazed how much distance you cover each year with your exercise routine.

What to Wear When Exercising

What you wear when you exercise is important because clothing will provide protection from the weather, depending on where you live.

- Shoes are probably the most overlooked item when beginning an exercise program. Unfortunately, many individuals begin with an old pair of sneakers they have had in the garage or closet for several years. Old shoes will not provide the support you need when exercising and can cause orthopedic problems such as soreness in the feet, knees, hips or lower back.

   If you are doing exercises that involve being on your feet, then you should make sure your shoes have good support and fit properly. Unfortunately, the support in shoes breaks down fairly quickly. Although the shoe may look almost new, the support that your body needs from the shoe may be gone. So the bad news is that you need to replace your shoes frequently. If you are exercising five days a week, you should probably replace your shoes at least every six months.

Buying cheap shoes or shoes in discount places is probably not a good idea. Purchase your shoes at a store where you can receive expert advice about the type of shoe you may need and then have it fitted properly. For the most part, consider wearing the type of shoe called the cross-trainer, which is made for a variety of physical activities such as walking and jogging. When fitting the shoe, make sure the expert watches you walk to look at your gait (how you walk), because some shoes are designed to make your feet turn in or turn out. If the shoes don't match your gait, then those shoes will cause you great discomfort. Special activities such as tennis, basketball, racquetball and aerobic classes require deck or court shoes.

The bottom line is that you could end up with shoes in your closet that still look good but have very little support. Here is one tip on what to do with the broken down shoes: Give them to the Salvation Army or similar charity. Don't use them to cut the lawn or some other activity because once again they could cause some orthopedic problem because the support is gone!

■ Clothing also provides protection to your body when you are exercising.

• In a cold environment, the layered approach works well when exercising outside. The first layer of clothing against your skin should be an item made of polyester and polypropylene fabrics because it will not absorb the sweat. Don't use clothing made of cotton

for the inner layer. Cotton will absorb sweat
and keep the moisture against your skin,
which interferes with the body's cooling
process. A polyester and polypropylene
fabric will allow the moisture to be wicked
away from the skin to the next layer, which aids
in regulating the body temperature even in a cold
environment. The other layered items should be
lightweight and consist of no more than three layers,
including the first layer against the skin. Too often,
you end up overdressing when exercising in a cold
environment. Remember that your body generates
heat when you exercise, so you will warm-up quickly,
even when outside in a cold environment.

The outer layer of clothing should be a good
windbreaker. It also should breathe to help dissipate
your body heat and eliminate perspiration. Gortex is
an excellent material for the windbreaker. There are
other materials on the market that also work very well
in dissipating body heat and eliminating perspiration.

Protecting the head in a cold environment is critical.
About 60 percent of your body heat is dissipated via
the scalp. A cap or stocking hat will prevent the loss
of too much body heat. Protecting the
head keeps you warm during an outdoor
activity in the cold. In extremely cold
weather, the ears need to be protected
from frostbite.

Protecting the hands is also very important. You need to worry about frostbitten fingers in extremely cold weather.

Ideally, you should wear mittens as opposed to gloves. Mittens keep the heat in one area and the fingers together, which helps fingers keep each other warm. Gloves separate the fingers and it is more difficult to keep them warm that way. Some individuals wear socks on their hands instead of gloves. Socks will work.

Protecting the feet is critical too. Insulated shoes or boots will keep the feet warm. Sometimes an extra layer of socks will do the job. But remember, an extra layer of socks could cause a tight fit  with your shoes and that could cause a problem such as blisters and restricted blood flow to the feet. Like the hands and ears, toes are susceptible to frostbite.

 Protect your eyes from the wind and snow. Glare from snow can be very dangerous to the eyes. Wear sunglasses or tinted goggles to protect your eyes from the glare and cold.

If you are going to be riding a bike in a cold environment or moving quickly outdoors such as downhill skiing or cross country skiing, you might want to purchase outdoor clothing items that will deflect the wind. Cycling pants for the cold are made to deflect the wind from the front of the legs. You can also purchase wind deflectors for the feet and hands and a mask for the face. If you don't wear a mask, purchase a gel or lotion to protect the facial skin from the extreme cold. The skin on your face, especially the cheeks, is susceptible to frostbite! Don't forget, when you are riding your bike in the cold you have to consider not only the temperature but the impact of the wind when riding at various speeds. This is also true with downhill skiing.

Don't be foolish when it comes to cold weather. Being outdoors in the cold can be fun and healthy. But it is not smart to go outdoors to exercise in extreme cold (when the temperatures are in the teens and the wind chill is in the single digits). Under these conditions, select an indoor physical activity until the cold passes. This is especially critical for young children.

- In a warm environment, you should dress to allow as much heat to escape from the body as possible. White clothing tends to deflect the sun. In most cases, a single layer of clothing is appropriate. The clothing should be made of a nylon type of material, which allows for perspiration to be wicked away from the skin. Cotton  absorbs the perspiration, which keeps the moisture against the skin, so cotton is not recommended. The warm breezes will allow the moisture from the nylon material to evaporate, which aids in regulating your body temperature. If you are bald, you might need to wear a cap or sunblock to protect your scalp. But select a mesh cap that will breathe and is light in color.

Protecting the feet from blisters is important in a hot environment. The heat from the pavement can cause blisters to occur. Make sure your shoes fit well and that you wear comfortable cotton socks.

If it is sunny, protect your exposed skin, including the scalp for bald heads, with a sun block of SPF 30 or greater.

Protect your eyes from the sun with good sunglasses. Sunglasses that wrap around the eyes and temples are the best.

What about Water Consumption When Exercising?

Fluid intake is important when exercising! Water is the best fluid to consume. If you are walking, you can always carry a  water bottle with you or you can purchase a fanny pack that will hold a bottle of water so you don't need to carry it. But no matter what kind of physical activity you are doing, water should be consumed on a regular basis. Don't wait to become thirsty! Even when doing  chores around the house, drink water. Stay away from alcoholic beverages when exercising or doing anything physically demanding, such as cutting the grass or working in the garden. Also, avoid caffeinated drinks such as iced tea or soft drinks. Caffeine is a diuretic and may increase water loss, which can increase the probability of becoming dehydrated.

Electrolyte solutions (such as Gatorade) are not necessary for most exercise regimens.

They will not cause any harm but sometimes the sugar in them will cause stomach discomfort. Consuming too much of a sugar solution will slow down the absorption process of the fluid into the digestive system. If you prefer electrolyte solutions, then dilute them with water, which will make them easier to be absorbed and cause less discomfort in the stomach.

 Make sure your children drink plenty of water each day. If your children are active (and we hope they are), encourage them to drink plenty of water, fruit juices (not fruit drinks) and low fat milk. Children perspire and can lose a good proportion of their body fluid rather quickly (much faster than an adult). This can cause them to become dehydrated much faster than an adult, which can be very dangerous!

An Exercise Holiday!

 Sometimes the best thing you can do for your body is take a holiday from exercise. Take a day off, giving your body some time to recover and repair itself. We suggest that you do this one or two days a week.

Children and Exercise!

Chapter 12 will be devoted entirely to children and how to get them involved in a variety of physical activities early in their lives. Unfortunately, many parents forget that their children are children and not small adults. Many times they impose adult exercise standards on children. Your child's body is smaller than yours, has less muscle and his or her bones are not fully developed. Remember, they are still growing and developing. It is more important, at an early age, to encourage your children to be physically active through play. Taking them to a park so they can run and climb on playground equipment encourages physical activity and play. Taking your children for a walk, bike ride or hiking are all good activities. But remember, they can't walk or ride their bike as fast as you. Also they cannot walk or ride the same distance that you would normally walk or ride.

Children are not miniature adults! Children are children. Everything that is expected of an adult in terms of physical activity needs to be diminished or reduced for children. The entire third section of this book is devoted to children, physical activity and nutrition and it begins with Chapter 11.

Chapter 4:

How Important Is Weightlifting to Achieving a Healthy Body Weight?

Much has been written over the past five years about the importance of weightlifting or strengthening exercises. Prior to that, much of the exercise emphasis focused on doing aerobics or continuous moving exercises to increase the fitness of your heart. Very little emphasis was placed on muscular strength.

Recent research clearly shows that individuals from all age groups and both genders can dramatically enhance their health by lifting weights or doing some form of strengthening exercises on a regular basis.

Here Are a Few of the Benefits:

■ Increased Protein (muscle) Metabolism.

When your protein metabolism is increased, you burn more calories! Strengthening exercises not only help you to keep your muscles strong, but they help you to lose weight while preventing the loss of muscle. This is very important since when most people diet, they not only lose fat weight, but they also lose muscle weight. Maintaining your muscle mass is critical, especially as you get older. Remember that in Chapter 2 we discussed the resting metabolic rate (RMR). As you age, you tend to lose muscle and gain fat, which slows your RMR. This means you burn fewer calories each day. This is why some people gain weight after the age of 50 even if they don't eat more.

The ideal weight loss program not only includes a reduction in calories consumed each day but also an exercise program that includes strengthening exercises. Adding weightlifting activities to your weight reduction program not only burns more calories (because of increased protein metabolism) but helps to maintain your muscle mass – and in some instances add to it, which is good.

■ **Protection for the Joints**

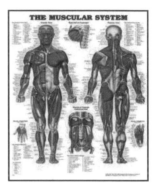

Muscle plays a critical role in supporting and protecting your joints – knees, shoulders, back and so on. Keeping the muscles strong not only allows you to per-form daily activities and sporting activities more efficiently, but also protects the joints from injury. This is critical for older individuals, especially if they slip or fall.

■ **Stronger Bones**

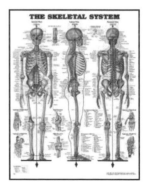

Recent research shows that weight-lifting not only prevents calcium loss from bone but also will increase the uptake of calcium into bone. This makes the bone stronger and plays a very important role in preventing osteoporosis. Obviously this is why weightlifting is an important activity for women. But the weight or resistance you lift must be substantial enough to present some difficulty without causing harm. This is critical in order to stimulate bone growth and calcium uptake into the bone. It is important to include many upper body activities (arms and shoulders) in your weightlifting routine to ensure the bones supporting the arms, shoulders, neck and upper back remain strong and healthy.

■ Children Grow up Stronger and Healthier

For many years, researchers felt children should not lift weights because of poten-tial damage to their bones while they are still developing. But recent research shows that children can become involved with weight training pro-grams if they don't involve lifting heavy weights. Most importantly, parents are  encouraged to let their children get involved with upper body activities that include climbing activities such as the use of playground equipment like monkey bars.

Selecting the Right Program

A great deal of scientific research has been done on what is the right amount of weightlifting to make a difference in your level of physical fitness. The authors are not going to delve into all of that research. If you are an elite athlete or want to go into athletic competition, then we suggest you purchase a book on weightlifting. This book is focusing on weightlifting designed to increase or maintain muscle strength and muscle mass and to increase the number of calories burned or expended each day.

Most weightlifting programs consist of repetitions and sets.

The number of times you perform the exercise repr
number of repetitions. It is usually suggested that you lift a
weight 8 to 12 times, then rest. Each group of 8 to 12 repetitions represents a set. The most common weightlifting program
consists of three sets of each exercise with one to two minutes
of rest between sets.

Amount of Weight to Lift

Using 8 to 12 repetitions for one set as a
guide, the amount of weight you select to lift
should allow you to do at least eight repetitions
with the 11th and 12th repetitions providing
some difficulty. Initially, you might be able to complete only
nine repetitions before the weight becomes too heavy to lift.
That is okay. With time, you will become stronger and be able to
complete 12 repetitions. Once you can complete 12 repetitions,
then it is time to add more weight. How much weight is added at
that time will depend on the exercise being performed. It might
be a couple of pounds or it could be more. But you add enough
weight to at least allow you to do eight repetitions again.   It is
critical to use a weight or resistance that is substantial enough to
reap the benefits described previously.

A similar workout strategy can be used for your child. The
main difference is that children under the age of 12 should lift
lighter weights with more repetitions. Their program would
consist of doing 12 to 16 repetitions for one set. The program
should consist of three sets. Chapter 12 discusses in more detail
strength training for children.

Rest between Sets

Lifting weights can provide some aerobic fitness. The rest between sets determines whether you will add an aerobic component to your strength workout. The shorter the rest time, the more you contribute to your aerobic fitness at the same time you are adding to your muscular strength. Some individuals allow only a few seconds between sets thereby maintaining an elevated heart rate from one exercise to the next. Rests up to two minutes allow for the heart rate to decrease, which takes away from the aerobic component. No matter which way you decide to do your strengthening exercises, you will still realize the strength benefits described above. Sometimes it is good to mix and match. Some days add the aerobic component and other days do just the strengthening component. Note that when you add the aerobic component with very little rest between sets, you might have to reduce the weight lifted, especially when you do the second and third sets, because of fatigue.

A note of caution: If you are just beginning, it is recommended that you take two minutes of rest between sets. As you progress with your strength conditioning program, you can begin to shorten the rest period between sets and begin to add alternatives to your routine such as the aerobic component.

Some individuals will do a strength exercise and then add an aerobic exercise before doing another strengthening exercise. For example, do an arm curl and then walk in place for 30 seconds. If you are working out in a fitness facility, you could do a strengthening exercise on one of the machines and then walk one lap around the track or hop on a stationary bike and pedal for one minute.

Sequence of the Exercises

There are a couple of routines to follow when doing strengthening exercises.

The first involves completing all three sets of the same exercise before moving on to the next exercise (standard routine). An alternative to this routine is to do one set of each exercise and then repeat the sequence two more times. The research shows that both routines are beneficial. The alternative routine makes it easier to add the aerobic component. You might want to alternate between these two routines. Use the standard routine one day and then the alternative routine the next time you work out. Look at the example below involving three different strengthening exercises.

Standard Routine	Alternative Routine
Leg Press – All Three Sets	Leg Press – Set One Chest Press – Set One Arm Curls – Set One
Chest Press – All Three Sets	Leg Press – Set Two Chest Press – Set Two Arm Curls – Set Two
Arm Curls – All Three Sets	Leg Press – Set Three Chest Press – Set Three Arm Curls – Set Three

Sometimes it is asked if it is important to exercise one part of the body first before doing another. At the level of strength training that is recommended with this book, the answer is no. Some individuals like to start with large muscle groups such as the legs and trunk first and then move to the shoulders and arms.

Number of Times Each Week

You should have at least one day of rest between workouts that involve strengthening exercises. Skipping a day between strength workouts allows the muscle to rebuild. Remember, one of the benefits of a strength-training program is increased protein metabolism. This means that muscle breaks down during strength training exercises and the muscle needs time to rebuild to become stronger. This is why it is recommended to skip a day between workouts. We suggest that you lift weights no more than three times a week. This pattern forces you to skip two consecutive days once a week. Research clearly shows that lifting weights three days a week will provide you with all the benefits discussed previously.

Safety First

Before we identify specific exercises, there are several key safety principles that must be followed or else you run the risk of injuring yourself.

First, never hold your breath while lifting a weight. This will increase the pressure in the chest and abdominal cavity, which could cause light-headedness or even fainting.

Also, this will greatly increase your blood pressure, which is not healthy, especially for those individuals with high blood pressure. Holding your breath while exercising is even more dangerous as you grow older.

Second, never do an exercise that causes pain – especially a sharp pain. This is indicative of a health problem that should be evaluated immediately by the appropriate medical authority. There is a fine line between joint or muscle pain and muscle soreness or stiffness that naturally occurs when you first start a weightlifting program. Muscle stiffness or soreness will end in a couple of days, and it does not prevent you from performing an exercise.

Third, always be aware of your surroundings. You do not want to do your weightlifting program in an area where you could cause harm to others or yourself because of close proximity to other individuals or objects. Make sure you have room to move freely through the full range of motion.

Fourth, always warm-up before beginning the weight-lifting program and always cool-down by stretching following the weightlifting program. The purpose of the warm-up and cool-down has been discussed in Chapter 3. Stretching exercises are identified below.

Fifth, make sure the object you are lifting is secure. You do not want the object you are lifting to come loose or break during the lift.

Sixth, be careful of some weight machines. They may cause harm to a joint. For example, the seated knee extension machine could put undo pressure on the knee joint and cause damage to the integrity of the knee.

Getting Started:

- In your home, weightlifting exercises can be done with dumbbells or they can be done by using plastic shopping bags (like the ones received from a grocery store) with handles and using canned food for the resistance. Make sure equal weight is placed in each bag. Resistance can be increased or decreased by using different sized cans or number of cans. Most of the strengthening exercises are done to a count. Sometimes it is a two count and other times it is a four count. For example, with arm curls, as you lift the weight it is done to a two count. You would count to yourself 1,001 and 1,002. When the weight is returned to the starting position, you do the same count – 1,001 and 1,002.

If you elect to use dumbbells, you should have several different sets to choose from. It is suggested that you have three, five, eight and ten-pound sets (two of each). As you become stronger and need more resistance, you can always purchase additional sets of dumbbells that weigh more. Dumbbells are reasonably priced and can be purchased in most local sporting goods stores.

- Other forms of strengthening exercises may include calisthenic exercises, stretch/elastic bands and weighted balls. Calisthenic exercises may involve more or fewer repetitions since with some calisthenic exercises the body weight needs to be lifted (i.e. push-up).   With calisthenic exercises, you usually complete the maximum number of repetitions possible (assuming the number is less than 20) and then complete three sets.

- If you belong to a fitness center, a fitness specialist can instruct you on a strength program. It should include a variety of the strength machines and dumbbells.

- Always perform the exercise in a controlled and slow motion during both phases of the lift. The actual lift is one phase and returning to starting position is the second phase.

Description of Various Strengthening Exercises

- **Weighted Knee Squats – thigh muscles, front of hips, buttocks, back of thigh**

  1. Start with back straight and knees extended. Hold weighted plastic bags in both hands at your sides.
  2. Lower body by bending at the knees. Keep back straight. Lower body until the thighs are no lower than parallel to the floor. Keep the weights still. Keep knees in line with toes. Four count down.
  3. Move body to start position, keeping the back straight at all times. Keep the weights still. Two count up.

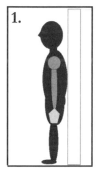
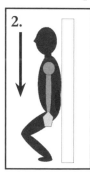
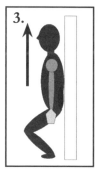

■ Weighted Leg Curls – back of thigh and buttocks

1. Start with body straight and weighted plastic bag around one foot. Hold on to wall for balance and support.
2. Keep body straight. Move heel of weighted foot to buttocks by bending knee. Two count up.
3. Return weighted foot slowly to the floor. Four count down.

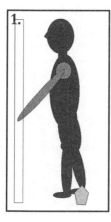 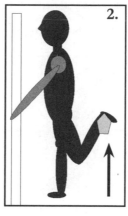 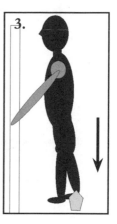

■ Weighted Knee Raises – thigh muscles, front of hips

1. Start with back straight and leg straight raised slightly off floor. Place weighted plastic bag over foot. Keep uninvolved leg slightly bent.
2. Lift leg upward into a bent-knee position. Lift as high as possible toward chest. Keep foot at a 90-degree angle. Two count up.
3. Move leg to start position by slowly lowering leg. Keep foot at 90-degree angle. Four count down.

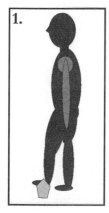 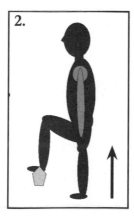 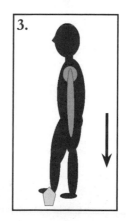

■ Weighted Leg Swings – thigh muscles, back of thigh, buttocks

1. Back straight and leg extended slightly above floor. Place weighted plastic bag on foot. Swing leg forward, keeping weight under control at all times. Keep uninvolved leg slightly bent.
2. Keep foot at 90-degree angle. Slowly swing leg behind you, keeping the leg straight. Control the weight at all times.
3. Return to start position and repeat movement. Keep the exercise leg straight. Keep the back and hips still.

Note: For balance, hold on to a countertop or back of a chair.

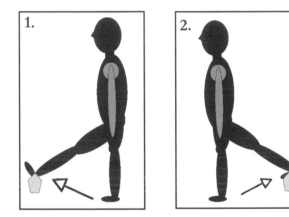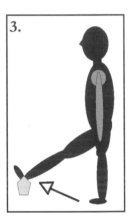

■ Bent Over Row – upper back

1. Start with arms straight, holding weighted bags, body forward, back flat, knees slightly bent.
2. Pull weighted bags to chest, bending elbows and shoulders – squeeze shoulder blades together. Two count up.
3. Slowly return to start position, keeping back flat and knees slightly bent. Four count down.

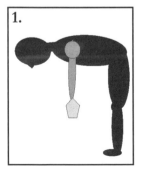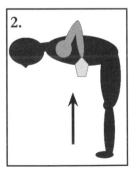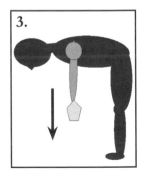

■ Shoulder Press – shoulders and upper back

1. Start with weighted bags at shoulders. Arms bent at elbows. Back flat and knees slightly bent.
2. Press weighted bags straight up by straightening the arms. Do not lock the elbows. Two count up.
3. Slowly return to start position, keeping back flat. Four count down.

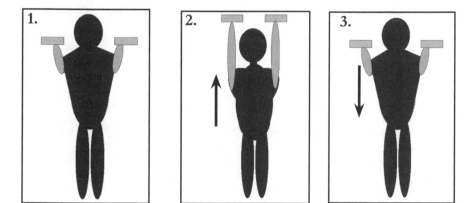

■ Front Raises – front of shoulder and back of shoulder

1. Start with weighted bags at side, arms straight, back flat, knees slightly bent.
2. Keep arms straight, move weights forward no higher than parallel to floor. Do not lock elbows. Two count up.
3. Slowly return to start position. Keep arms straight, back flat, knees slightly bent. Four count down.

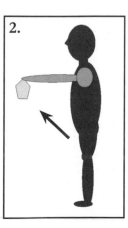
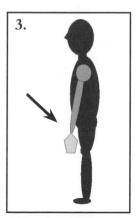

■ **Lateral Raises – middle of shoulder, upper back**

1. Start with weighted bags at side, feet shoulder-width apart, back flat, knees slightly bent.
2. Raise arms to the side – parallel to floor. Two count up.
3. Slowly return to start position. Keep arms straight. Two count down.

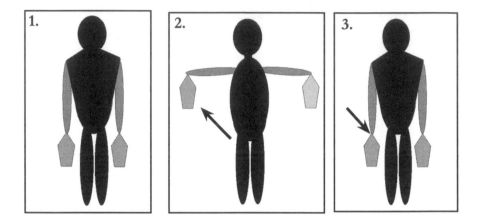

■ **Curls – front of upper arm**

1. Start with weighted bags at side and arms straight. Back flat, knees slightly bent.
2. Bend at elbows, lift weight to shoulder. Keep back flat. Two count up.
3. Slowly return to start position. Four count down.

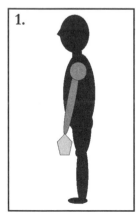
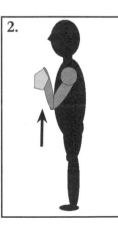
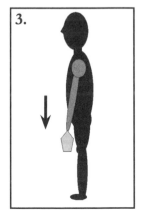

Description of Various Calisthenic Exercises

■ **Push-ups – back of upper arm, chest, upper back**

1. Start prone position, body slightly off ground, back straight, hands shoulder–width apart.
2. Keep body straight, push against floor, raise body to full extension of arms.
3. Slowly return to start position. Don't let body touch the floor.

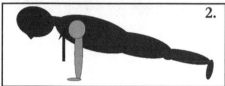

Alternative is to place hands more than shoulder-width apart - uses more chest.

■ **Dips on a Chair – back of arm, upper back and shoulder**

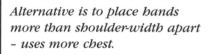
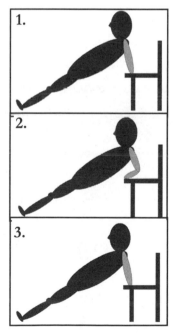

1. Start body straight in supine position, arms straight and hands placed on chair, feet on floor. Do not lock elbows. Make sure chair is secure so it won't tip.
2. Bending at the elbow, slowly lower your body, keeping it straight. Lower yourself to the chair. Keep elbows facing back of chair. Four count down.
3. Slowly return to start position, keeping body straight. Two count up.

Beginner: Start with knees bent at right angle.

Advanced: Place feet on chair same height as chair for hands. More difficult to do.

■ **Abdominal Curls – stomach area**

1. Start prone position, arms across chest, knees bent, feet flat on floor.
2. Lift upper body by curling the trunk, abdominal area. Raise trunk to 45-degree angle. Keep arms across chest.
3. Slowly return trunk to the floor by uncurling the trunk. Keep arms across chest. Four count down.

Alternative – during up phase, twist the trunk. Alternate right/left with each curl.

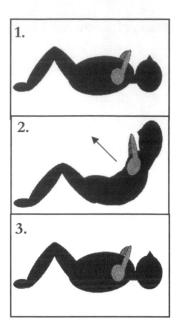

Description of Stretching Exercises

Stretching can be done in conjunction with an exercise routine or independently to help relieve tension and stress. It is always a good practice to stretch as part of your warm-up and cool-down. Always perform a stretch according to the following stretching principles:

- Slowly move to a point of slight discomfort and then hold the stretch for **15 seconds**.
- Slowly release the stretch and return to the starting position.
- Repeat the stretch up to three times.
- Never bounce or move quickly.
- If a stretch causes pain, stop immediately.

Many individuals will stretch in the morning following a warm shower. Others stretch before crawling into bed at night. You should stretch every day at least once a day. Some individuals have an orthopedic problem such as low back pain. With orthopedic problems, stretching may help to relieve the discomfort and aid in the healing process. But always check with your doctor before doing any exercise.

The following stretches are an example of what can be done. The examples show stretches that cover most of the muscle groups in the body. You may know of others, which is fine. But no matter which stretch you do, always follow the stretching principles stated above.

■ **Side of Neck – rotating**

1. Sit or stand with arms hanging loosely at sides.

2. Slowly turn head to one side and hold.

3. Slowly return to starting position and slowly turn head to other side and hold.

■ **Side of Neck – bending**

1. Sit or stand with arms hanging loosely at sides.

2. Slowly tilt head sideways to one side and hold.

3. Slowly return to starting position and slowly tilt head to the other side and hold.

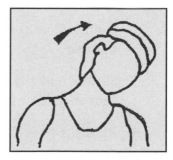

■ **Back of neck**

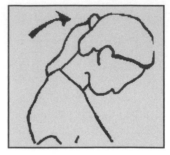

1. Sit or stand with arms hanging loosely at sides.

2. Gently tilt head forward to stretch back of neck and hold.

■ **Back of shoulder and upper arm and upper back**

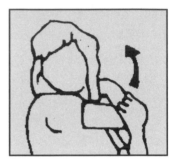

1. Stand or sit and place right hand on left shoulder.

2. With left hand, pull right elbow across chest toward left shoulder and hold.

3. Repeat for other side, reversing hand and arm positions.

■ **Back of arm, shoulder, side of body and waist**

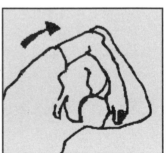

1. Stand or sit with arms overhead.

2. Keep knees slightly flexed.

3. Hold one elbow with hand of opposite arm.

4. Slowly pull elbow behind head gently as you slowly lean to side until mild stretch is felt and hold.

5. Repeat by reversing positions of arms.

- **Calf – back of lower leg**

  1. Stand a short distance from wall and lean on it with forearms, head resting on hands.

  2. Place right foot in front of you, leg bent, left leg straight behind you.

  3. Slowly move hips forward until you feel stretch in calf of left leg and hold.

  4. Keep left heel flat and toes pointed straight ahead.

  5. Repeat by reversing positions of legs.

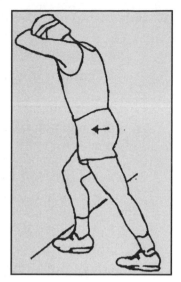

- **Front of Upper Leg – thigh**

  1. Stand a short distance from wall and place left hand on wall for support.

  2. Standing straight, grasp top of left foot with right hand.

  3. Slowly pull heel toward buttock and hold.

  4. Repeat by reversing hand and leg positions.

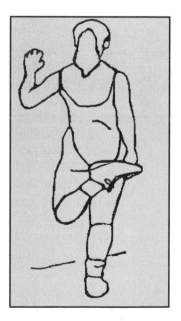

■ **Side of hip and back of thigh**

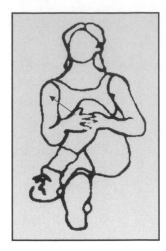

1. Sit on floor with right leg straight out in front.

2. Bend left leg, cross left foot over right leg, place outside right knee.

3. Slowly pull left knee across body toward opposite shoulder and hold.

4. Repeat by reversing the hand and leg positions.

■ **Lower back, side of hip and neck**

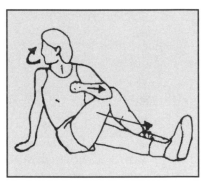

1. Sit on floor with left leg straight out in front.

2. Bend right leg, cross right foot over left leg, place outside left knee.

3. Bend left elbow and rest it outside right knee.

4. Place right hand behind hips on floor.

5. Slowly turn head over right shoulder, rotate upper body to the right and hold.

6. Repeat by reversing hands, legs and head.

- **Back of leg and lower back**

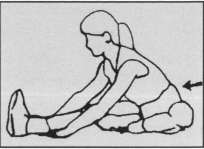

1. Sit on floor, legs straight out and spread apart as wide as possible.

2. Bend left leg in at knee.

3. Slowly bend forward from hips toward foot of straight leg until you feel slight stretch and hold.

4. Do not dip head forward at start of stretch.

5. Keep foot of straight leg upright, ankles and toes relaxed.

6. Use a towel if you cannot easily reach your feet. Place the towel around the sole of your foot and pull yourself toward the foot by holding on to the ends of the towel.

7. Repeat, by reversing positions of legs.

Keep a Log of What You Do

Keeping a log of what physical activity you do on a weekly basis allows you to monitor physical activity progress and accomplishments. The chart on page 69 (a blank one can be found in the Appendix that can be duplicated and used to keep track of your physical activities or you can download a copy by going online to www.moveitloseitlivehealthy.com) shows one version of how to track all of your physical activity, including major chores. Even if an activity does not occur, it is logged as "off" or "no" for the day. Strengthening exercises are normally tracked by logging the number of sets, repetitions per set and weight used. If the activity is a calisthenic exercise, such as push-ups or abdominal curls, then the number of sets and repetitions are recorded. Time and distance are normally logged for cardiovascular activities. Keeping track of the stretches that you do is also important. Monitoring major chores such as cutting the grass (assuming you are walking behind the lawn mower), gardening, housework and similar activities also helps you to realize the amount of physical activity in one day.

By using the blank form in the Appendix, you can set up several physical activity routines to add variety to your workout or to take into consideration seasonal changes. Planning a physical activity routine helps you to achieve it. Or you can keep several logs – one for strength exercises, one for cardiovascular, one for stretching and one for chores. Another way to track your physical activity is to record the steps you take each day. See the month of April in Chapter 14 for information on pedometers.

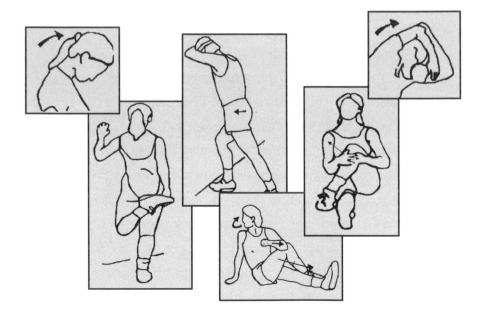

Exercise Type	Date 7/1/04	Date 7/2/04	Date 7/3/04	Date 7/4/04	Date 7/5/04	Date 7/6/04	Date 7/7/04
Strength	Sets/ Reps/Wt	Sets/ Reps/Wt	Sets/ Reps/Wt	Sets/ Reps/Wt	Sets/ Reps/Wt	Sets/ Reps/Wt	Sets/ Reps/Wt
Shoulder Press	2/12/20	Off	2/12/20	Off	2/12/20	Off	Off
Forward Raises	2/12/10	Off	2/12/10	Off	2/12/10	Off	Off
Chest Pulls from Bent Position	2/12/15	Off	2/12/15	Off	2/12/15	Off	Off
Weighted Knee Squats	2/12/30	Off	2/12/30	Off	2/12/30	Off	Off
Curls	2/12/5	Off	2/12/5	Off	2/12/5	Off	Off
Weighted Leg Curls	2/12/30	Off	2/12/30	Off	2/12/30	Off	Off
Calisthenics	sets/reps	sets/reps	sets/reps	sets/reps	sets/reps	sets/reps	sets/reps
Push-ups	2/20	2/20	2/20	2/20	2/20	2/20	2/20
Abdominal Curls	2/20	2/20	2/20	2/20	2/20	2/20	2/20
Cardiovascular	Dist/Time	Dist/Time	Dist/Time	Dist/Time	Dist/Time	Dist/Time	Dist/Time
Walking	2 mi. 35 min.	No	2 mi. 35 min.	No	2 mi. 35 min.	No	Off
Biking	No	6 mi. 40 min.	No	6 mi. 40 min.	No	6 mi. 40 min.	Off

Exercise Type	Date 7/1/04	Date 7/2/04	Date 7/3/04	Date 7/4/04	Date 7/5/04	Date 7/6/04	Date 7/7/04
Stretching							
Tricep, shoulder	Yes	Yes	Yes	Yes	Yes	Yes	Yes
Middle back	Yes	Yes	Yes	Yes	Yes	Yes	Yes
Calf, achilles	Yes	Yes	Yes	Yes	Yes	Yes	Yes
Hamstring	Yes	Yes	Yes	Yes	Yes	Yes	Yes
Lower back	Yes	Yes	Yes	Yes	Yes	Yes	Yes
Sports							
Tennis		60 min.			60 min		
Chores							
Cut Grass			40 min.				
Gardening						30 min.	
House Cleaning	30 min.		30 min.		30 min		90 min.

You have now read about the importance of physical activity and how to put into place a routine that meets your needs. Physical activity is critical to achieving and maintaining a healthy body weight.

Highlights – Physical Activity Section

You now have completed reading the section on physical activity. To make sure you understand the critical components of body weight management and physical activity, we have highlighted several points that should be the focus of your physical activity program. Following each statement is the page number where you can find additional information.

1. Obesity is an epidemic in the United States. Most research shows that at least 60 percent of the American population is either overweight or obese.
    Page 8

2. Your weight is controlled by calories! It is that simple. The food consumed is measured in calories, which can also be referred to as energy intake. All of your body's activities, from your heart beating to riding a bike, can be measured in calories, too. This is your energy output or expenditure. Your energy output is divided into two components – energy for routine daily activities and energy for physical activity or exercise such as riding a bike, walking or playing a sport.
    Page 16

3. If the number of calories that you consume each day is less than the number of calories expended, you will lose weight over time.
    Page 17

4. Although controlling your body weight does seem simple, the body makes it much more difficult. Located in

the brain is a nerve center that acts to control your body weight by controlling your hunger. The body has a "set point" controlled by this nerve center that keeps our body weight fairly constant – even though your weight can be too much, too little or just right. The set point doesn't like change, especially rapid change, because the body likes to remain in balance or "homeostasis." The set point can be altered but only through small, gradual changes. Small changes help maintain a sense of "homeo- stasis" or balance, which the body will accept.
Page 19

5.   One item that does impact your body weight as you grow older is your "resting metabolic rate" (RMR). The RMR is the amount of energy needed to sustain your daily activi- ties – the heart to beat, lungs to breathe, working, eating, driving a car and so on. RMR tends to slow down as you age. So what daily adjustments should you make to your lifestyle after the age of 50?
  • consume slightly *fewer* calories, or
  • increase your physical activity level, or
  • keep as much muscle as possible through a strength training program, or
  • all of the above!
Page 21

6.   Today, it is important to include as much physical activity in your daily routine as possible. The American College of Sports Medicine now encourages individuals to partici- pate in at least 30 minutes of moderate physical activity five days a week. The good news is that the 30 minutes can be divided into segments and it does not have to take place in a fitness center. It can occur in your home,

in your neighborhood, at the mall, in your backyard – and it includes any physical activity you do at work!
Page 23

7.   When your protein metabolism is increased, you burn more calories! This could help prevent adding weight to your body as you grow older. Strengthening exercises not only help you to keep your muscles strong, but they help you to lose weight while preventing the loss of muscle. This is very important since when most people diet, they not only lose fat weight, but they also lose muscle weight. Maintaining your muscle mass is critical, especially as you get older. Remember that on page 21 we discussed the resting metabolic rate (RMR). As you age, you tend to lose muscle and gain fat, which slows your RMR. This means you burn fewer calories each day. This is why some people gain weight after the age of 50 even if they don't eat more.
Pages 26, 47

8.   When starting an exercise program, the key word is *"gradual."* Everything involved in your physical activity program should be done *gradually*. The length of time of your exercise program should increase gradually. Changes to your exercise routine should be done gradually. The speed (intensity) at which you do the exercise should increase gradually.
Page 30

9.   The warm-up prepares your body for the actual physical activity. The actual activity should last from 15 minutes to an hour. The cool-down allows the heart to slow down gradually, return to its pre-exercise level and for

the muscles to be stretched again. These are the three components to an exercise routine.
Pages 30 - 31

10. Many people think the more exercise done (if one hour is good, then two hours must be twice as good) and the faster it is done, the quicker their bodies will become physically fit. It doesn't happen that way. That approach to a physical activity program will result in injury to the body.
Page 33

11. Using 8 to 12 repetitions for one set as a guide, the amount of weight you select to lift should allow you to do at least eight repetitions, with the 11th and 12th repetitions providing some difficulty.
Page 50

12. Never hold your breath while lifting a weight. This will increase the pressure in the chest and abdominal cavity, which could cause light-headedness or even fainting. Also, this will greatly increase your blood pressure, which is not healthy, especially for those individuals with high blood pressure.
Pages 53 - 54

Section Two

A Common Sense Approach to Nutrition

Chapter 5:
Good Nutrition and Healthy Eating-A Tricky Balancing Act

Over the last several chapters, we have spent considerable time on how to get moving and the importance of burning calories to help us maintain a healthy body weight. In the next several chapters, we are going to discuss the other side of the equation, the number of calories consumed and the food we eat or drink.

If Number of Calories Consumed Is Less Than Number of Calories Expended,

You Lose Weight!

In addition to discussing the food we eat or drink, this chapter will also discuss the importance of a balanced diet and what is meant by a balanced diet.

The Body Likes to Be in Balance

The body likes "homeostasis" – to be in balance. The body does not like extreme or radical changes. Changing your diet too quickly is extreme. Fad diets are extreme. You lose weight quickly by eliminating essential food groups or by adding certain foods. Extreme changes are not healthy for your body. The body is very complex. Every day thousands and thousands of chemical reactions take place in the body. These are very normal reactions, but most importantly, they are extremely critical to our everyday bodily functions.

For example, did you know:

- The heart needs calcium and potassium to function. Diets that restrict calcium or potassium consumption put not only the heart but many normal bodily functions at risk!

- The body needs a certain amount of cholesterol in its diet to provide a critical covering (myelin) for our nerves. Without cholesterol, the myelin sheath could become unhealthy. For this reason alone, nutrition experts do not recommend restricting fat for children under two years of age. This could have a negative impact on many normal bodily functions.

- Carbohydrates are the body's main source of energy. We need carbohydrates to have the energy to work, play and for normal bodily functions to occur. Restricting carbohydrates severely would be very unhealthy to the body.

The body needs critical nutrients every day such as carbohydrates, protein and fats. Also, there are many essential vitamins and minerals that are needed to make it possible for thousands of chemical reactions to occur each day in our bodies. Restricting any group of foods could deprive the body of critical vitamins and minerals, which would upset or even alter these chemical reactions, thus having a negative impact on your "homeostasis."

Are you willing to upset this critical balance (homeostasis) just to lose some pounds quickly when, in the long run, the loss could be very damaging to your body and your health?

So, the smart approach is to monitor the calories eaten each day and to make sure the calories come from a balanced diet.

> If your goal is to lose weight, it should be done by reducing the number of calories eaten each day in conjunction with an increase in daily physical activity. The weight loss should be gradual and based on a goal of two to three pounds a month.

Choosing a Balanced Diet!

Choosing a balanced diet does not have to be difficult. Good, healthy eating involves eating a variety of foods each day. Food provides our bodies with energy and the ingredients to grow and maintain body cells. Carbohydrates, protein and fat are the main ingredients or nutrients needed by our bodies. A properly balanced diet should consist of 50-60 percent as carbohydrate, 15-20 percent as protein and 25-30 percent as fat. For example, a 2,000 calorie diet would be:

55% carbohydrate	1,100 calories (.55 X 2,000) or 275 grams (carbohydrate @ 4 calories per gram)
20% protein	400 calories (.2 X 2,000) or 100 grams (protein @ 4 calories per gram)
25% fat	500 calories (.25 times 2,000) or 56 grams (fat @ 9 calories per gram)

Carbohydrates, protein and fat provide calories for our bodies. Carbohydrates and fat are the primary sources of energy. Protein can supply energy but its main function is for the growth and maintenance of body tissue. Notice that one gram of carbohydrate or protein equals four calories while one gram of fat equals nine calories.

How Many Calories Do You Really Need Each Day?

Wouldn't it be wonderful if you could esti-
mate the number of calories you need to con-
sume each day? (Check out www.mypyramid.
gov.) And then, based on that information, you
could determine if you need to decrease the
number to lose weight or increase the number
to gain weight. Or, if your goal is to keep things on an even
keel, keep eating the same number of calories.

The next three chapters take a look at the main food ingredients of a balanced diet – carbohydrates, protein and fat.

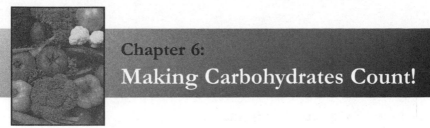

Chapter 6:
Making Carbohydrates Count!

Carbohydrates are the body's main source of energy. They are the body's source of fuel. They are like gasoline for a car. Without gasoline, the car doesn't run. The body is no different. Without carbohydrates the body won't run, or if it does it is running on only half of its cylinders! Foods with carbohydrates also are good sources of essential vitamins and minerals.

Examples of foods that supply carbohydrates naturally are breads, rice, pasta, fruits, vegetables (including legumes – dried beans and peas), milk and yogurt. Carbohydrates are easily digested by the body and broken down into glucose, which is the primary source or form of energy accepted by our body cells. Carbohydrates not used immediately as energy are stored as glycogen in the muscle. Once the glycogen stores reach their capacity, the extra glycogen is stored as fat, primarily in our fat cells, as a triglyceride.

There are some sources of carbohydrates that contain a large portion of refined or added sugar such as soft drinks, fruit flavored drinks, desserts, sweets, syrups and jams. Sugar has also found its way into most processed foods

including soup, condiments like ketchup, spaghetti sauce, canned fruits, cereals and frozen dinners.

A Few Words about Sugar

How much sugar is in the food you con-
sume? To find out, read the ingredient informa-
tion on the food label for sugar content. Sugar
comes in many forms on the ingredient list.
Take a look at the list below to get some idea of
some of the various forms of sugar.

- corn syrup
- honey
- molasses
- cane sugar
- confectioner's sugar
- dextrose
- fructose
- glucose
- lactose
- maltose

Food labels list grams of sugar per serving as well as grams of total carbohydrate. Keep in mind that one teaspoon of white table sugar = four grams of carbohydrate. One gram of carbohydrate equals four calories. So one teaspoon of sugar consumed is equal to 16 calories (four grams times four calories).

How can you make good use of this information? On the food label, sugar information is given based on one serving size. Let's say that the food label states one serving has 20 grams of sugar. If you want to know how many calories this is, multiply the total number of grams of sugar by four. In this case one serving of sugar has 80 calories.

Sugar tastes good and is hard to resist. However, too much sugar can add a considerable number of calories to your daily diet if you are not careful.  Just imagine if you consumed four glasses of iced tea each day and each glass of tea had three teaspoons of sugar added. For breakfast, you add one teaspoon of sugar to your cereal and later in the day you add one teaspoon of sugar to a bowl of strawberries. What does this all add up to?

Iced Tea	12 teaspoons (4 glasses times 3 t)
Cereal	1 teaspoon
Strawberries	1 teaspoon

All tolled, you added 14 teaspoons of sugar to your daily diet, which means you consumed 224 calories (14 teaspoons times 16 calories) from sugar. This does not take into consideration sugar found in other foods you consumed. You can see that at this rate it doesn't take long before you begin adding to your waistline. This makes it very difficult to maintain a healthy body weight.

For this reason you may want to consider the use of sugar substitutes or a low caloric sweetener to provide some sweet flavor without giving the extra calories. There are many types of low calorie sweeteners on the market. The Food and Drug Administration (FDA) has approved the use of saccharin, aspartame, acesulfame potassium and sucralose.

- Saccharin can be used in hot and cold foods.

- Aspartame (NutraSweet) is often used in cold foods because high temperatures decrease its sweetness. Because aspartame contains phenylalanine, it should not be used by persons with PKU (phenylketonuria – a rare disease).

- Acesulfame potassium (Sweet One) can be used in baking and cooking. However, it may affect the texture of baked goods. Cooking tips from the manufacturer can help to improve your baking results.

- Sucralose (Splenda) can be used as sugar in any food product. It too can result in altered texture in baked goods. Following the manufacturer's baking suggestions will help.

Relying on low calorie sweeteners can help to eliminate some excess calories from your diet, but using these products should not be a reason to deviate from a healthy diet. Daily use of low calorie sweeteners is not recommended for children, except for children with diabetes.

Using small amounts of refined sugars in your diet can enhance your meals and be enjoyable. The tendency of most people is to use too much sugar. Besides lacking necessary vitamins and minerals, the excess sugar results in excess calories, which can add fat to the waistline. Let's compare an 8 oz. serving of various beverages. (See chart on page 85).

Beverage	CHO* (grams)	Calcium (mg)**	Potassium (mg)	Vit C (mg)	Calories
Cola	26	7	3	0	104
Diet Cola	0*	14	0	0	1
Kool-Aid	20	0	9	6	80
Lemonade	27	71	34	8	102
Punch	29	20	62	73	120
Orange Juice	27	20	480	96	112
Apple Juice	29	17	295	2	116
Milk, Fat Free (Skim)	12	301	407	2	86
Milk, Whole	11	290	371	2	150
Milk, Chocolate, 1 %	26	288	425	2	158
Milk, Chocolate, Whole	26	280	418	2	208
Tap Water	0	5	0	0	0

*If less than 0.5 gram, calculated as zero (0); CHO = carbohydrates
**mg=milligrams
Note: Food values obtained from <u>Bowes & Church's, Food Values of Portions Commonly Used,</u>
18th edition, Lippicott Williams and Wilkins

When comparing these beverages, their carbohydrate content is about the same - except for the whole and skim milk, diet cola and water. But what about the nutrient value? Sugar-laden drinks such as cola, Kool-Aid, lemonade and punch are considered empty calorie foods because they provide very little nutrient value. They have calories, which can quickly add up to weight gain, but they bring very little nutritional value to the body. Also, many people today substitute sweetened beverages for water. Water has no carbohydrates or calories but brings great value to the body. What's your choice going to be? A naturally sweetened drink packed with vitamins and minerals, such as fat-free milk or orange juice, or an added-sugar sweetened drink with almost no nutritional value, such as cola? To achieve a healthy body weight, selecting a naturally sweetened drink would be healthier than selecting an added-sugar sweetened drink as long as their calories are taken into account. Too much "good-for-you" beverages can add up to extra pounds also.

Fiber

Fiber is another type of carbohydrate. It is an indigestible substance found in certain foods. Fiber has been in and out of the news for the last ten years because it lowers blood cholesterol and possibly protects against colon cancer.

For adults, the amount of fiber recommended for each day is 25-35 grams. This sounds like a lot but it really isn't because fiber comes in different forms and from different foods. There are two types of fiber with different benefits. Some groups of foods may have more than one kind of fiber.

■ Soluble fiber is found in oat bran, oatmeal,  legumes (dried beans and peas), lentils, barley, apples, pears, strawberries, citrus fruits and psyllium. Psyllium is a grain found in cereal products, dietary supplements and bulk laxatives. Read food labels for psyllium. This type of fiber is helpful in lowering blood cholesterol and in controlling blood sugar, as well as improving bowel regularity.

■ The other type of fiber is called insoluble fiber. Good food sources of insoluble fiber include wheat bran, cereals with wheat bran, whole grain breads, vegetables and select fruits. Insoluble fiber also helps  with bowel elimination and can help prevent bowel or intestinal problems.

■ *Note: Meat, milk, cheese, yogurt without fruit, plain ice cream, sugar, fats, oils and margarine contain no fiber.*

One very important thing to keep in mind when increasing the amount of fiber in your diet is to drink plenty of fluids, particularly water, to help the body move the fiber through the intestinal system.

If you are interested in losing weight, work to include some high fiber foods in meals and snacks because they help to fill you up and in most cases are low in calories. (A real win-win choice for your weight loss program).

Here's how a few foods stack up when it comes to fiber content:

Fiber Content		
4 or more grams	**1 to 3 grams**	**Less than 1 gram**
1/2 cup cooked dried beans or peas (kidney, large lima, navy, pinto, black-eyed), soybeans	1 slice whole wheat, pumpernickel, rye or cracked wheat bread, 1 bagel, rye crispbread, large English muffin, white pita bread, 1 medium tortilla	Whole wheat pancake, 1 slice white bread, 1 biscuit, melba toast, taco shell, wonton wrapper, pancake, white dinner roll
1/2 cup cooked lentils	1/2 cup canned applesauce, apricots, cherries, fruit cocktail, peaches, pears, pumpkin, pineapple	1/2 cup white rice, rice noodles, egg noodles, water chestnuts, canned mushrooms, green peppers, canned mandarin oranges, grapefruit, grapes
1 cooked artichoke, 1 medium mango, pear, persimmon	1 medium apple, banana, kiwi, orange, peach, tangerine, nectarine, passion fruit	2 graham crackers
1/2 cup raspberries or blackberries, raisins	1/2 cup fresh strawberries, blueberries, cranberries	4 saltine crackers
	4 prunes	fruit juice

4 or more grams	1 to 3 grams	Less than 1 gram
Certain whole grain breads and cereals (check food label): 1 rye triple cracker, 1 large whole wheat pita bread	1/2 cup cooked asparagus, broccoli, Brussel sprouts, cabbage, carrots, celery, cauliflower, corn, mushrooms, eggplant, green beans, kale, okra, potatoes, plantains, spinach, squash, sweet potatoes, tomatoes, turnips, yams, zucchini and whole wheat noodles	1 cup melon, iceberg lettuce, alfalfa sprouts, 1 medium plum
	2 TB rice or wheat bran, wheat germ, whole wheat flour, soy flour	
2 dried figs	2 dates or fresh figs	
	4 whole wheat	crackers
	1/2 grapefruit	
2 TB* flaxseeds	1 oz. mixed nuts**, sunflower seeds, corn chips, potato chips, 2 TB peanut butter or sesame seeds, 2 oz. tofu	1 oz. pretzels, 1 cup popped popcorn
	Certain cereals (check food label)	

* TB = Tablespoon

**1 oz. peanuts=28, 1 oz. pecans=20 halves

Note: Fiber content information obtained from <u>Bowes & Church's, Food Values of Portions Commonly Used</u>, 18th edition, Lippicott Williams and Wilkins

Glycemic Index (GI)

Before we move on to another important food nutrient, it is important to briefly discuss the Glycemic Index (GI). Although the GI has been known and discussed in the dietary profession for many years, it has recently begun to be recognized as a better means to classify carbohydrates. Why? Because of the role carbohydrates play in association with diabetes. Now that diabetes has reached an epidemic state in the United States and other countries, carbohydrates are being closely scrutinized.

What is the relationship between carbohydrates and diabetes? The concern is that eating too many carbohydrates that have a high Glycemic Index (greater than 60) can increase the body's demand for a larger production of insulin. (Insulin is secreted by the pancreas. It enables our body's cells to absorb glucose to be used for energy and to maintain a normal glucose level.)

When we eat large amounts of foods that produce a high glycemic load over and over and over again, there is a continual presence of high insulin levels in the body. This has been directly linked to a higher incidence of Type II diabetes, heart disease and certain cancers.

What is the Glycemic Index? It is the rate at which the body converts carbohydrates into blood sugar and how high the blood sugar climbs. For example, white bread is digested almost immediately into glucose, causing the blood sugar to rise quickly. So white bread would have a high GI. On the other hand, milk or

 legumes take longer to digest, causing the blood sugar to rise more gradually and therefore have a lower GI rating. In terms of the body and its response to blood sugar levels, it is healthier to have blood sugar levels rise gradually than to spike quickly. This is easier on the pancreas and provides more control of insulin in the blood, which may reduce the body's risk for diabetes.

Carbohydrate foods are compared to a GI base number of 100. This is the Glycemic Index number assigned to the ingestion of pure glucose. So other GI numbers, assigned to carbohydrates, are based on the rate to convert the carbohydrate to sugar in comparison to pure glucose. As a result, most, if not all, the index values for carbohydrate foods are below 100. The further the number is below 100, the healthier the carbohydrate.

Nutritionists are still debating what is a healthy GI. Is it below 40 or 60 or 80? What is the overall impact on the GI when you consume a combination of carbohydrates that have both low and high GI values?

 As mentioned earlier, even though the Glycemic Index has been around for many years, not many foods have been rated according to their GI rating. This limits the use of the GI at this time, but more is being learned every day and more and more foods are being rated with a GI. We have included in the Appendix a website to check for a list of foods with their GI ratings. You will note foods such as fats and protein are not listed because they contain very little carbohydrate.

The tricky thing about the GI is how it impacts recipes that contain more than just carbohydrates or multiple carbohydrates. The GI number can be affected by the combination with other foods, where it was produced and the recipe used to produce it. The Glycemic Index probably has its best application when considering the consumption of a single carbohydrate when nothing else is consumed. For example, eating a candy bar, cookie or a piece of bread. The use of the GI along with other foods, which normally occurs in a meal, diminishes the importance of the GI. For example, potatoes along with a meat and another vegetable greatly diminishes the significance of the GI for potatoes. The potato, in this instance, has less of an impact on the release of insulin than when consumed by itself.

In order to use the Glycemic Index to help regulate your diet, a good rule is to consume a variety of foods, limiting the amount of refined and highly processed carbohydrates, and try to include food choices with a low GI number. For instance, instead of having a soft drink with a meal, drink fat free (skim) milk instead. When making soup, include some black beans or navy beans or both! Sprinkle a few nuts on a salad. Choose fresh fruit for snacks and dessert instead of pies, ice cream and candy. Remember that subtle changes, when put into place for long periods of time, result in significant weight loss and tremendous health gains!

There is much more to learn about the Glycemic Index and the glycemic load of foods. This is just another piece to a complex puzzle. It is recommended that a variety of foods, from all the food groups, be selected each day in order to include foods with high fiber content and limit the amount of poor nutrient, high calorie foods like soft drinks, candy, cookies, cake, chips and highly processed foods.

The Brown Bag Lunch, Carbohydrates and Fiber

So let's compare two brown bag lunches (page 94) to see what just a few simple changes can do in terms of carbohydrate, fiber and calorie consumption.

Brown Bag A is a typical lunch – a lot of carbohydrates, very little fiber and too many calories.

Brown Bag B substituted whole wheat bread for the white bread and used less mayonnaise, added fruit and raw vegetables and a smaller portion of potato chips. Brown Bag B also exchanged the soft drink with a bottle of water.

These changes resulted in 129 grams of fewer carbohydrates, or 512 fewer calories from carbohydrates for Brown Bag B. Because of less fat and sugar consumed, the total calories with Brown Bag B were 895 fewer consumed than with Brown Bag A.

Brown Bag B is a healthier lunch and accounts for about 25 percent of your total calories for a 2,000 calorie daily diet. This allows for enough calories for breakfast, dinner and mid-morning and afternoon snacks. By changing to whole wheat bread and adding fresh fruit and vegetables, the fiber content reaches ten grams, which is 1/3 – 1/2 of the adult recommended intake for the day!

With subtle changes like this in your diet, you are well on your way to achieving a healthy body weight.

Brown Bag A	CHO* (grams)	Fiber (grams)	Calories
Turkey Sandwich:			
2 slices white bread	24	1	134
2 oz. turkey breast	0	0	64
2 teaspoons mayonnaise	0	0	66
1 teaspoon mustard	0*	0*	3
3 oz. potato chips	45	3	456
Apple turnover	65	2	420
20 oz. soft drink	65	0	260
Total	**199**	**6**	**1403**
Brown Bag B			
Turkey Sandwich:			
2 slices whole wheat bread	26	4	138
2 oz. turkey breast	0	0	64
1 teaspoon mayonnaise	0	0	33
1 teaspoon mustard	0*	0	3
3 slices tomato	3	1	13
4 fresh spinach leaves	0*	0*	1
1 oz. potato chips	15	1	152
1 medium fresh apple	19	2	73
1/2 cup baby carrots	7	2	31
20 oz. bottled water	0	0	0
Total	**70**	**10**	**508**

*If less than 0.5 gram, calculated as zero (0); CHO = carbohydrates
Note: Food values obtained from <u>Bowes & Church's, Food Values of Portions Commonly Used,</u> 18th edition, Lippicott Williams and Wilkins

Chapter 7:
Keeping Protein in Proportion

Protein is another very important nutrient required by our bodies. Dietary protein is used for growth, repair and the daily renewal of body tissues. Protein is a major constituent of our bodies as part of muscle, bones and connective tissue. Even our hair, nails and skin are made of protein. Protein can also be found in certain blood components such as albumin, enzymes and some hormones.

Essential Amino Acids

Protein is made of components called amino acids. There are 22 amino acids identified in the body. Nine of these are referred to as "essential amino acids." The reason for this is that they are not produced by our bodies and must come from our diets. Animal protein foods contain all nine essential amino acids and are therefore called complete protein sources. Examples of these include milk, cheese, eggs, yogurt and meat.

This is another prime reason why fad diets or unbalanced diets can be harmful to your health. They may lack these essential amino acids. Vegetarians, too, must be careful to balance protein in meals, particularly for children!

Plant protein sources such as vegetables, fruit and grains do not contain all essential nine amino acids. Protein in plant foods may lack one or more of the essential amino acids and are called incomplete proteins. High protein plant sources include nuts, seeds, legumes, lentils and tofu.

One way to make sure you get all the essential amino acids when eating plant protein instead of animal protein is to combine the plant protein with a grain food source (plant source) or another animal protein source in the same meal. For example, peanuts provide the amino acid that is lacking in grain products. So the combination of peanut butter and bread (preferably whole grain bread) makes the peanut butter sandwich a perfect combination to equal a complete protein or meat substitute.

Plant Protein + Grain or Complete Protein = Meat Substitute with All Essential Amino Acids

For example, the following combinations will provide you with the essential amino acids:

Red Beans	+	Brown Rice
Peanut Butter	+	Whole Wheat Bread
Chopped Nuts	+	Yogurt
Black Beans	+	Corn

Getting Enough Protein

Getting enough protein for most people is not the problem. We usually get more than is actually needed. Let's take a look at some protein sources. Note the portion listed. For example, one ounce of meat provides seven grams of protein.

Food Item	Protein (grams)
1 oz. meat	7
1 oz. cheese	7
1 egg	7
8 oz. milk	8
8 oz. yogurt	8
1 slice bread	2
1/2 cup rice or pasta	2
1/2 cup cooked cereal	2
1/2 cup vegetable	2
1 cup leafy vegetable	2
1/2 cup cooked legumes	7
Large baked potato w/butter	4
1 cup green salad	2
2 rolls	4

The Typical American Meal – What a Difference a Portion Makes

Let's compare the protein intake and calories from a typical American meal to the exact same meal only using smaller portions. You will be amazed as to what happens to the calories consumed.

Typical Portion Sizes for a Meal:

Food Item	Protein (grams)	Calories
12 oz. Grilled Steak (about 9 oz. cooked)	63	675
Large Baked Potato w/ 3 pats butter	5 0	202 108
Large Green Salad 3 TB Salad Dressing	1 0	25 75
2 Rolls	4	160
12 oz. Soft Drink	0	144
Totals	73	1,389

Note: Food values obtained from <u>Bowes & Church's, Food Values of Portions Commonly Used,</u> 18th edition, Lippicott Williams and Wilkins

Looking at a typical American meal and assuming the goal for the number of calories required each day is 2,000 calories, it is easy to see how you can gain weight.

■ The typical American meal shown in the above table shows you would consume 73 grams of protein and 1,389 total calories.

■ The calories consumed account for nearly 70 percent of your daily calorie count in just one meal.

■ The 73 grams of protein consumed is equal to 292 calories.

- Only 400 calories in protein would be required for the day. This means nearly 75 percent of your protein requirement would be consumed in this one meal.

- What would have happened to the total calories if a dessert were tacked on?

By the way, the excess protein consumed each day, that the body does not need, is metabolized by the body and stored as fat.

Smaller Portion Sizes for a Meal:

Food Item	Protein (grams)	Calories
6 oz. Grilled Steak (about 4 1/2 oz. cooked)	32	338
Medium Baked Potato w/1 pat butter	4 0	135 36
Medium Green Salad 2 TB Salad Dressing	0 0	17 50
1 Roll	2	80
12 oz. Skim Milk	12	120
Totals	50	776

Note: Food values obtained from Bowes & Church's, Food Values of Portions Commonly Used, 18th edition, Lippicott Williams and Wilkins

A few simple modifications can make a significant difference in the calories consumed. The difference in calories consumed between these two typical American meals is 613 fewer calories for the meal with smaller portions.

- When compared to your total calorie requirement of 2,000 calories, the smaller portion meal accounts for only 39 percent of your total calories, in comparison to the same meal with larger portions, which accounts for nearly 70 percent of your daily calorie requirement. You consume the same food but less of it.

- Also, the protein is reduced from 73 grams to 50 grams, or a difference of 23 grams. Instead of consuming 75 percent of your protein requirement with larger portions, you are now consuming 50 percent.

- This also means that other meals and snacks during the day can be used to meet your protein and calorie requirement.

Imagine what would happen to your body weight simply by consuming smaller portions each day. The net result would be significant weight loss – a good and smart way to achieve a healthy body weight.

We have discussed making small, subtle changes. Perhaps making all the changes shown on the smaller portion meal above are too many for you. What if you just consumed one roll a day instead of two and used two tablespoons of salad dressing instead of three? That is a caloric savings of 105 calories. One hundred five calories a day for an entire year is 38,325 calories for the year. This will result in a weight loss of about 11 pounds. By the way, using smaller portions most of the time means that once in a while you can splurge and have dessert!

By making a few minor adjustments in the portion sizes consumed each day, you are well on your way to achieving a healthy body weight.

Chapter 8:
Fitting Fat into Your Diet!

Saturated, polyunsaturated, monounsaturated, cholesterol, trans fatty acids, omega-3 fatty acids, good cholesterol, bad cholesterol...these terms are so confusing. What do they all mean? And how can you keep them all straight?

Actually, when talking about fats, it's all about chemical structures...bonds and double bonds with carbon atoms and so on. It is how the fats are made or structured that determines how our bodies react to them.

Fat is a concentrated energy source and is essential to our bodies. We need a minimum of 25-35 grams of fat each day. Fat is used for the absorption of the fat-soluble vitamins A, D, E and K. Caution: With no fat in the diet, these vitamins are not absorbed.

In food, there are two primary types of fat: saturated and unsaturated. A saturated fat has no double bonds and an unsaturated fat has at least one. The chemical structure of the fat determines whether a fat is monounsaturated (one double bond) or polyunsaturated (more than one double bond). Most foods contain both saturated and unsaturated fats. Depending on the food, one of these two fats will be more dominating than the other.

Saturated fats raise blood cholesterol levels and LDL (low density lipoproteins). Whenever possible, foods that contain saturated fats should be avoided. The following list shows the food sources that have the highest amounts of saturated fats:

1. coconut oil – 87% of fat is saturated
2. butter fat – 63% of fat is saturated
3. palm oil – 49% of fat is saturated
4. lamb fat – 46% of fat is saturated
5. beef fat – 41% of fat is saturated
6. pork fat – 38% of fat is saturated
7. chicken fat – 30% of fat is saturated

Coconut oil and palm oil are often referred to as tropical oils and are frequently used in processed foods. You have to read the ingredient list on the food label very carefully to find them. Butter fat is found in dairy foods like whole milk, cream, sour cream and cheese. Would you believe that butter fat is higher in saturated fat than pork fat? Well, that is true.

Monounsaturated fats may help lower LDL. Fats that contain monounsaturated oils are healthier for you. Look for foods that have these oils on the food label:

- canola oil
- peanut oil
- olive oil
- some fish oils
- Avocados are another good food source of monounsaturated fat.

Polyunsaturated fats tend to lower LDL but too much of them can also decrease HDL (high density lipoprotein). Polyunsaturated fats are healthy for you (if you don't overdo it). Foods that contain the following oils are sources of polyunsaturated fats:

- safflower oil
- corn oil
- cottonseed oil
- sunflower oil
- sesame oil
- soybean oil

Nuts and some seeds are a great source of protein and also contain polyunsaturated and monounsaturated fats. See the table below for some nut and seed sources and the predominate type of fat they contain.

Polyunsaturated	Monounsaturated
Brazil Nuts	Almonds
Pine Nuts	Cashews
Pumpkin Seeds	Filberts
Walnuts	Macadamias
Sesame Seeds	Peanuts
Sunflower Seeds	Pecans
Flaxseeds	Pistachios

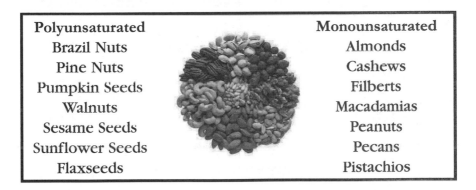

Omega-3 Fat

Some fish contain a polyunsaturated fat called omega-3. Salmon, halibut, sardines, lake trout, mackerel, herring and albacore tuna are all good sources of omega-3. Other good sources are canola and flaxseed oil.

Omega-3 fat has been found to lower blood triglycerides, decrease growth of plaque in arteries, decrease risk of arhythmias and lower blood pressure slightly. These  changes will contribute to a healthier cardiovascular risk profile.

Some people take fish oil tablets in order to get more omega-3 fat. Too much of some supplements can affect blood clotting mechanisms and can be harmful. For these reasons, you should consult your doctor before taking supplements such as fish oil. Some fish oil supplements may contain contaminants or toxic levels of vitamin A.

As with any dietary supplement, get the facts from the experts before proceeding.

A Few Words about Fish Safety for Women and Young Children

Even though fish and shellfish provide many nutritional benefits, the consumption of too much fish may represent a health hazard for women who may become pregnant, are pregnant or breastfeeding and for young children. This health hazard is due to mercury found in fish and has resulted in a warning issued by the EPA (Environmental Protection Agency) and the FDA (Food and Drug Administration) of the United States. Basically, all fish and shellfish contain some mercury resulting from the mercury contamination found in the environment. Fish absorb the mercury and over time it builds up in their systems. Intake of high levels of mercury can affect the developing nervous system of the unborn baby or young child.

The EPA and FDA fish consumption guidelines for women who may become pregnant, are pregnant or breastfeeding and for young children are:

- Do not eat shark, swordfish, king mackerel, or tilefish.

- Limit fish intake to 12 oz. per week. Choose fish with lower mercury levels such as shrimp, canned light tuna, salmon, pollock and catfish.

- Due to higher levels of mercury in alba-core tuna, limit the intake of this type of tuna to 6 oz. per week (about 1 cup, drained). (Canned light tuna has less mercury.)

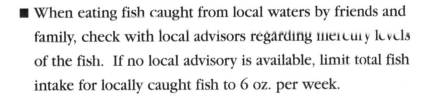

- When eating fish caught from local waters by friends and family, check with local advisors regarding mercury levels of the fish. If no local advisory is available, limit total fish intake for locally caught fish to 6 oz. per week.

Cholesterol

Cholesterol has received a lot of bad and unfair press over the last ten years. As a result, many individuals try to avoid foods with cholesterol. Well, keep this in mind: Cholesterol is an important part of our bodies. The body has the ability to pro-duce cholesterol in addition to what is ingested from our diet.

Cholesterol is critical to the maintenance and function of certain tissues in the brain and nervous system. It is needed, for example, for vitamin D to be absorbed and for various hormones and bile acids (required for digestion) to be formed. However, when the amount of cholesterol in the blood gets too high, it increases our risk of heart disease.

Organ meats – such as liver, kidney and brains – and egg yolks are high in dietary cholesterol. In fact, only foods of animal origin can contain cholesterol. All meats have cholesterol. Butter, cream, cheese and lard also have cho-  lesterol. Logically, you would expect foods high in cholesterol to raise blood cholesterol but that is not always true. The culprit in raising blood cholesterol is saturated fats. Certainly, it is a good idea not to eat large amounts of high cholesterol foods. But do keep in mind that dietary cholesterol does not appear to raise blood cholesterol as much as saturated fat.

Check out the cholesterol and saturated fat values of a few foods from the chart on page 109.

Experts advise that the daily diet be kept to 300 mg per day of dietary cholesterol. By viewing the table on page 109, you can see why. Minimizing the organ meats, such as liver and egg yolks, makes it easier to accomplish this goal. Careful planning can allow these high cholesterol foods to be eased into the diet occasionally, particularly if you are keeping the saturated fat content low.

Food	Cholesterol (milligrams)	Saturated Fat (grams)
3 1/2 ounces:		
Prime rib, lean only	81	8
Liver	389	2
Chicken, dark meat, no skin	93	3
Bologna	63	7
Salmon, baked	86	2
Boiled shrimp	193	0.2
Cheese	105	21
1 Egg yolk	272	2
1 Egg white	0	0
8 oz. whole milk	34	5
8 oz. skim milk	4	0.3

Note: Food values obtained from Bowes & Church's, Food Values of Portions Commonly Used, 18th edition, Lippicott Williams and Wilkins

Note that cholesterol is measured in milligrams and saturated fat is measured in grams. 1,000 mg = 1 gram. For example: to make a fair comparison, saturated fat needs to be expressed in milligrams. When that is done for the prime rib, the saturated fat would be 8,000 milligrams versus 81 milligrams of cholesterol. You can see from these examples, most foods with fat contain much more saturated fat than cholesterol.

Lipoproteins

Oh boy, here is another fat to worry about! Actually, lipoproteins are carriers. They are like cars. They carry the fat from one part of the body to another. Some are good in that they help get rid of fat, like cholesterol. Some are bad because they transport the fat to the arterial wall and deposit it there.

Over time, these fatty deposits increase your risk for a heart attack or stroke because they make it more difficult for blood to flow through the arteries. Usually your total cholesterol is made up mostly of LDL and HDL. (There are other lipoproteins to consider but we will not discuss them at this time.) Bottom line is the higher the LDL is relative to your total cholesterol, the higher your risk is for cardiovascular disease. In contrast, the higher the HDL is relative to your total cholesterol, the greater protection you have against cardiovascular disease.

LDL, HDL and other lipid components make up your total cholesterol. LDL normally makes up the largest component. But, the percentage of LDL and HDL can be altered to favor less risk for heart disease through dietary adjustments and increased levels of physical activity. As shown on page 111, the pie charts indicate what could happen to the percentage of LDL and HDL cholesterol following a lifestyle change. The "Total Cholesterol – After" is a much healthier cholesterol profile. In this case, the total cholesterol did not change (both pie charts are the same size) but the percentage of each component did. The HDL increased from 20 percent to 30 percent and the LDL decreased from 70 percent to 60 percent.

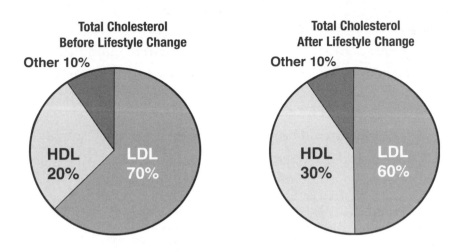

Total Cholesterol
Before Lifestyle Change

Other 10%

HDL
20%

LDL
70%

Total Cholesterol
After Lifestyle Change

Other 10%

HDL
30%

LDL
60%

- Low density lipoprotcins (LDL). These lipoproteins are associated with the bad or unhealthy cholesterol.

- LDL takes blood fat, primarily cholesterol, from the various tissues and deposits the fat on the walls of the arteries.

- As the fat builds up, the *lumen* or opening in the artery becomes smaller, a condition called *arteriosclerosis*.

- As the diameter of thc blood vessel decreases, it becomes more difficult for blood to travel through the artery.

- If the blood vessel becomes completely blocked, then the blood supply is cut off. If the artery leads to the brain, a stroke occurs. If the artery leads to the heart, a heart attack occurs.

- High fat foods eaten in excess, especially saturated fats, can increase the amount of LDL in the blood.

- *Trans fatty acids* have also been found to raise LDL levels. These are found (see next section) in foods that contain *hydrogenated* and *partially hydrogenated oils.*

- The following list gives you some idea as to the kinds of foods that would be high in saturated fat, which can raise LDL or bad cholesterol.

Milk Products	Meat Products	Other Food Items
Homogenized Whole Milk	Bacon	Coconut Oil
Regular Cheese	Sausage	Butter Fat (Milk Fat)
Cream	Spareribs	Palm Oil
Sour Cream	Hot Dogs	Lamb Fat
Cream Cheese	Luncheon Meats	Beef Fat
Ice Cream	Fat Trimmings From Meat Cuts	Pork Fat (Lard or Bacon Grease)
	Poultry Skin, Vienna Sausage or Deviled Ham, Potted Meat	Hydrogenated Oil
		Partially Hydrogenated Oil

- High density lipoproteins (HDL) are associated with good cholesterol. HDL keeps fat (cholesterol) from building up in your blood vessels by transporting cholesterol to the liver, where it is broken down and removed. The higher the HDL the less risk there is for cardiovascular disease.

- Foods generally don't influence HDL, except trans fatty acids, which will cause them to decrease (see next section).
- *Aerobic exercise* has the most influence on HDL. It will increase the amount of HDL in the blood.
- If an individual smokes, *quitting* will increase the amount of HDL.
- If an individual is overweight, *losing weight* can increase the amount of HDL.
- A lifestyle that maintains a healthy body weight, involves aerobic physical activities and no smoking is the best way to keep HDL high.

Trans Fatty Acids

If you have been listening to the news lately, it's likely that you have heard about trans fatty acids. But what are they? Basically they are oils, like soybean or corn oil, that have undergone a process called hydrogenation.

Hydrogenation makes the oil harden. It actually changes the chemical structure of the oil. As a result, the hydrogenated fat does not become rancid as quickly, allowing food with hydrogenated fat to have a longer shelf life. This means the food will last longer without going bad, but is that really healthy? It is the hydrogenation process that allows butter or margarine to be formed into a stick, or for peanut butter to be soft enough to spread instead of being a liquid.

That may make a food easier to use, but there are no health benefits from eating hydrogenated fat. Besides acting like a saturated fat, which raises our LDL (bad cholesterol), it also decreases

our HDL (good cholesterol). This presents double tr
our arteries. The arteries have more LDL to clog them and fewer
HDL to whisk away the LDL – a worst-case scenario in terms of
your health!

When reading the ingredient list on a food label, the terms to
look for are "hydrogenated" or "partially hydrogenated." When
you start reading ingredient lists, you may be surprised to find
these terms on just about every processed food that you eat,
including:

- microwave popcorn, crackers, cakes, doughnuts, cookies,
  chips, bread, muffins, pastries, pies, breaded chicken or
  fish and peanut butter.

And if the list includes shortening or margarine, then this is
another trans fatty acid food source. If you eat out, the list goes
on. Most restaurants (including fast food restaurants) use a hydrogenated-type oil in food preparation, including frying. In fact,
the only natural source of trans fatty acid is found in dairy and
beef fat – and their levels are low.

Take advantage of the trans fat information on food labels. As
of January 2006, Canada and the U.S. have laws requiring that
trans fatty acids be listed.

Check out foods that have opted **not** to use hydrogenated fat.
A good example is peanut butter – natural peanut butter, that is –
it's "just peanuts."

> Read the ingredient list and aim for low fat foods and those that use oil (not palm or coconut oil) instead of hydrogenated or partially hydrogenated fat. This will keep you away from foods that tend to increase your LDL or bad cholesterol.

Listed below are some healthy tips on how to **reduce** the amount of trans fatty acid in your diet:

- When eating out, choose foods that are steamed, broiled or grilled instead of fried.

- And if you must have dessert, choose something light, such as sorbet or low fat frozen yogurt with a fresh fruit topping, instead of a baked dessert such as pie, cake or pastry.

- You can also question restaurants about the type of oil they use. Don't simply settle for the response of "vegetable oil" but ask if it contains hydrogenated or partially hydrogenated fat.

- When shopping, choose a margarine that lists "liquid oil," such as liquid olive oil, liquid canola oil or liquid corn oil, as the first ingredient on the food label. (Remember that when reading an ingredient list, ingredients are listed in descending order. So the first ingredient is in the highest quantity in the product.)
  - Experts still recommend this type of margarine instead of butter.

- With the new labeling law now in effect, companies list trans fatty acids as "trans fat." Compare similar products when shopping and choose the one with less trans fat.

- In addition, some trans fat-free foods are being developed. So watch for these new products at the grocery. Even though reading labels is a time-consuming process at first, you will soon learn which are the healthy products to buy.

- When cooking at home, use oil instead of shortening or margarine when possible.

  - The authors highly recommend olive or canola oil. For example, if you are making a quick bread or muffins and the recipe calls for shortening, substitute an equal or slightly less amount of oil instead and add it to the mixture with the liquid ingredients.

- Pop popcorn the old-fashioned way in which *you* add the oil to the popcorn or try air-popped popcorn to eliminate the extra fat and calories. Remember, most microwave pop-corns contain trans fats, which increase your LDL levels and lower your HDL levels.

Avoiding trans fatty acids could be one of the best things you can do for your health. By eliminating trans fatty acids from your diet, you are limiting LDL (bad cholesterol) and many extra calories. Because of this, many people are also able to shave away a few extra pounds just by avoiding foods that contain trans fats.

Here Is a Healthy Heart Tip:

> Set a healthy heart goal for one month. Eliminate trans fats from your family's diet. Your entire family will benefit from this objective and you will find that it will be easy to continue even after the month is over. Oh, and by the way, we also suggest that you add a daily 15-minute family physical activity period. A real winning combination – fewer trans fats and more physical activity!

If you can follow four simple Fat Guidelines identified below, you will take a very important step toward lowering your blood lipids (LDL, cholesterol and triglycerides).

Fat Guidelines

- It is okay to consume some fat in each meal, but don't overdo it. Try to keep the intake low.

- Choose foods low in saturated fat and trans fatty acids – avoid the LDL foods.

- When choosing an oil, use canola or olive oil.

- When choosing margarines, salad dressings, mayonnaise and other foods that are primarily fat, make sure liquid canola and liquid olive oil are the key ingredients. If not, choose a product that contains soybean, peanut, sesame, corn, safflower, or cottonseed oil.

Compare Two Fast Food Meals – Fat Does Make a Difference

Here is an example of what could happen to your fat intake by simply making a few healthy changes as previously identified. Let's compare two takeout meals.

Fast Food Takeout Meal **One**	Fat (grams)	Fat Calories	Total Calories
1 large fried chicken breast	28	252	470
1 fried chicken drumstick	10	90	160
1/2 cup mashed potatoes w/gravy	6	54	120
1 corn-on-cob w/margarine	5	45	168
1 biscuit	10	90	180
1/2 cup peach cobbler	12	108	261
12 oz. soft drink	0	0	150
Total	**71**	**639**	**1509**

Fast Food Takeout Meal **Two**	Fat (grams)	Fat Calories	Total Calories
1 large fried chicken breast w/out skin	8	72	305
1/2 cup mashed potatoes w/gravy	6	54	120
1 corn-on-cob w/margarine	5	45	168
1 plain roll	2	18	80
1 medium fresh peach (from home)	0	0	42
12 oz. diet soft drink	0	0	1
Total	**21**	**189**	**716**

Note: Food values obtained from Bowes & Churches, Food Values of Portions Commonly Used, 18th edition, Lippicott Williams and Wilkins

Wow! What a difference the fat makes!

- Meal Two provides 50 fewer grams of fat or 450 fewer fat calories. Remember, one gram of fat is equal to nine calories.

- With Meal One, 42 percent of its total calories come from fat; whereas, Meal Two has only 26 percent of its total calories from fat.

- To get a visual picture, remember that 14 grams of fat = 1 tablespoon (TB). Meal One has 71 grams of fat or 5 TB of fat, compared to Meal Two with 21 grams of fat or $1^{1}/_{2}$ TB.

- The total calorie difference is significant. Meal Two has 793 fewer calories than Meal One.

If you frequently pick up meals at the fast food counter, ask for nutritional information on the foods offered. You can then be more selective by ordering foods with less fat and fewer calories.

You will see and feel the difference as your weight begins to drop and you come closer to achieving your healthy body weight.

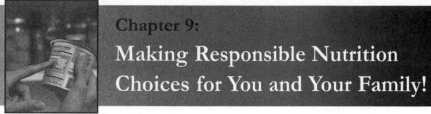

Chapter 9:
Making Responsible Nutrition Choices for You and Your Family!

Our daily life bombards us with many food choices that are available to us at a moment's notice. Think about it! Everywhere we turn, there is food. We can't get away from it. There are fast food restaurants on every corner, gas stations with numerous goodies, vending machines in the halls, TV commercials, grocery stores, magazines with attractive recipes and advertisements, and they all beg for our attention. There are new food products emerging daily to entice our appetites and dollars.

It is so tempting to indulge. And unfortunately for our health, that is exactly what we do over and over again until we are now in an obesity epidemic. On the other hand, there is the desire to be thin, so billions of dollars are spent annually on dieting, dieting gimmicks, quick result methods, and surgeries to undo our bad habits. It seems like we are in a no-win situation, or a catch-22!

It is time for a change! Change can happen when you decide that you want to be healthier and you want your family to be healthier too – a change that when done over time will result in permanent healthy lifestyle habits. So, where do you begin?

- The best way to know where to start in terms of your nutrition is by taking a good look at what you and your family are actually eating. It involves writing and recording all the food consumed over a three-day period. This is called a dietary record. If you find keeping a dietary record for three days is impossible, at least keep a record for one typical day.

- This may seem too time consuming to do. But remember, this is about you taking control of your health.

- It will be well worth the effort to keep the dietary record not only for yourself but for your children too! Why? Because our experience is that most individuals clearly underestimate the amount of food consumed each day.

- Even if you underestimate by just a mere 100 calories a day (one large chocolate chip cookie), the net result is the consumption of 36,500 calories more a year – or about 10 pounds in unaccounted added body weight.

So keeping a detailed dietary record of what you eat for at least three days is the best way to see what you are eating each day (see the sample dietary record chart in the Appendix or go to our website, www.moveitloseitlivehealthy.com, to download these charts for your use).

Many people will say, "I know what I eat. I don't have to write it down."

But writing down what you eat allows you to look over the day and evaluate where improvements in your diet are possible. It also allows you to set a plan of action to make small adjustments in your diet that will allow for permanent changes in your lifestyle. The potential benefits of this process far outweigh the effort it takes to complete the three-day dietary record.

To get an idea if what you are eating is balanced and within the calorie level needed, check out the MyPyramid Food Intake Pattern Calorie Level and MyPyramid Food Intake Patterns charts. The MyPyramid replaces the Food Pyramid that has been in use for many years. The United States Department of Agriculture (USDA) released the new dietary guidelines in April 2005.

MyPyramid

MyPyramid represents a personal nutrition and physical activity guide for persons of ages two and up. It serves as a reminder to encourage daily, and healthy lifestyle choices. MyPyramid is divided into six colorful food group bands, which suggest good health comes from eating a variety of foods daily. The bottom of the bands is wider than the top of the bands and represents types of foods that should be eaten more often. These are foods that contain a low amount or no solid fats (saturated and trans fat) and added sugars. Foods with higher fat and sugar content are represented at the top of the colored bands, which is the narrower portion of the band.

It is not important for you to memorize the MyPyramid.

- The purpose of discussing MyPyramid is to bring to your attention the importance of eating a variety of foods each day.

- Some are healthy foods and some are not.

- Our bodies need foods from each major food group every day, not just for the calories, but more importantly for the minerals and vitamins the body needs to sustain life.

MyPyramid Food Intake Pattern Calorie Levels

MyPyramid assigns Individuals to a calorie level based on their sex, age, and activity level.

The chart below identifies the calorie levels for males by age and activity level. Calorie levels are provided for each year of childhood, from 2-18 years, and for adults in 5-year increments.

Activity level	MALES		
	Sedentary*	Mod. active*	Active*
AGE			
2	1000	1000	1000
3	1000	1400	1400
4	1200	1400	1600
5	1200	1400	1600
6	1400	1600	1800
7	1400	1600	1800
8	1400	1600	2000
9	1600	1800	2000
10	1600	1800	2200
11	1800	2000	2200
12	1800	2200	2400
13	2000	2200	2600
14	2000	2400	2800
15	2200	2600	3000
16	2400	2800	3200
17	2400	2800	3200
18	2400	2800	3200
19-20	2600	2800	3000
21-25	2400	2800	3000
26-30	2400	2600	3000
31-35	2400	2600	3000
36-40	2400	2600	2800
41-45	2200	2600	2800
46-50	2200	2400	2800
51-55	2200	2400	2800
56-60	2200	2400	2600
61-65	2000	2400	2600
66-70	2000	2200	2600
71-75	2000	2200	2600
76 and up	2000	2200	2400

*Calorie levels are based on the Estimated Energy Requirements (EER) and activity levels from the Institute of Medicine Dietary Reference Intakes Macronutrients Report, 2002. SEDENTARY = less than 30 minutes a day of moderate physical activity in addition to daily activities. MOD. ACTIVE = at least 30 minutes up to 60 minutes a day of moderate physical activity in addition to daily activities. ACTIVE = 60 or more minutes a day of moderate physical activity in addition to daily activities.

United StatesDepartment of Agriculture Center for Nutrition Policy and Promotion April 2005 CNPP-XX

MyPyramid Food Intake Pattern Calorie Levels

MyPyramid assigns Individuals to a calorie level based on their sex, age, and activity level.

The chart below identifies the calorie levels for females by age and activity level. Calorie levels are provided for each year of childhood, from 2-18 years, and for adults in 5-year increments.

	FEMALES		
Activity level	Sedentary*	Mod. active*	Active*
AGE			
2	1000	1000	1000
3	1000	1200	1400
4	1200	1400	1400
5	1200	1400	1600
6	1200	1400	1600
7	1200	1600	1800
8	1400	1600	1800
9	1400	1600	1800
10	1400	1800	2000
11	1600	1800	2000
12	1600	2000	2200
13	1600	2000	2200
14	1800	2000	2400
15	1800	2000	2400
16	1800	2000	2400
17	1800	2000	2400
18	1800	2000	2400
19-20	2000	2200	2400
21-25	2000	2200	2400
26-30	1800	2000	2400
31-35	1800	2000	2200
36-40	1800	2000	2200
41-45	1800	2000	2200
46-50	1800	2000	2200
51-55	1600	1800	2200
56-60	1600	1800	2200
61-65	1600	1800	2000
66-70	1600	1800	2000
71-75	1600	1800	2000
76 and up	1600	1800	2000

*Calorie levels are based on the Estimated Energy Requirements (EER) and activity levels from the Institute of Medicine Dietary Reference Intakes Macronutrients Report, 2002. SEDENTARY = less than 30 minutes a day of moderate physical activity in addition to daily activities. MOD. ACTIVE = at least 30 minutes up to 60 minutes a day of moderate physical activity in addition to daily activities. ACTIVE = 60 or more minutes a day of moderate physical activity in addition to daily activities.

United StatesDepartment of Agriculture Center for Nutrition Policy and Promotion April 2005 CNPP-XX

- Consuming 2,000 calories a day from junk food (candy, chips, soft drinks) may be enough to keep you moving and alive but over time the body will suffer. It can actually become malnourished even with 2,000  calories a day if those calories are coming from foods that have empty calories. These are foods with no or minimal nutritional value.

- This is why it is important that you understand the concept behind MyPyramid. Use MyPyramid as a guide.

Okay, are you ready to compare your dietary record to MyPyramid? This is one way to make sure you achieve a body weight that is *healthy* for you.

- Look at the MyPyramid Food Intake Pattern Calorie Level chart on pages 128 and 129 and select the level that describes your age and activity level. You can go online at www.mypyramid.gov to determine your Intake Pattern Calorie Level based on your age, height, weight and activity level.

- The Food Intake Pattern Calorie Level chart can help you make a safe and healthy decision on what you need to do to lose weight. For example, to lose one pound per week, you need to generate a negative calorie balance of 3,500 calories. In other words, you need to burn 3,500 calories more than what you consume. One pound of fat is equal to 3,500 calories.

- What can you do to achieve this? Your daily calorie intake must be 500 calories fewer than what you expend (500 calories times seven days is 3,500 calories). This is best achieved by increasing your activity level and decreasing your calorie intake. So, if you are a 35-year-old male, who is Sedentary, the MyPyramid Food Intake Pattern Calorie Level chart shows that you need about 2,400 calories a day to maintain your current body weight. By increasing your activity level to Moderate, you now need 2,600 calories to maintain your current body weight.

  - If you increased your activity level to Moderate and kept your current caloric intake (2,400) the same, you would have a negative daily calorie balance of 200 calories. This is a good start, but you are still 300 calories short of the 500 you need to cut in order to lose one pound of fat each week.

  - What else can you do? You can increase your activity level to the next level (Active). But it is not a reasonable and healthy decision to move from a Sedentary lifestyle to an Active one. Remember in Chapter 3, we discussed the importance of gradually increasing our level of activity. So increase your activity level to Moderate and make up the difference by altering your diet – eliminate 300 calories each day from your diet. Instead of consuming 2,400 calories, consume 2,100 calories.

- Using the detailed dietary record you completed, compare your food choices to the MyPyramid Food Intake Pattern chart.

MyPyramid Food Intake Patterns

The suggested amounts of food to consume from the basic food groups, subgroups, and oils to meet recommended nutrient intakes at 12 different calorie levels. Nutrient and energy contributions from each group are calculated according to the nutrient-dense forms of foods in each group (e.g., lean meats and fat-free milk). The table also shows the discretionary calorie allowance that can be accommodated within each calorie level, in addition to the suggested amounts of nutrient-dense forms of foods in each group.

Daily Amount of Food From Each Group

Calorie Level	1,000	1,200	1,400	1,600	1,800	2,000	2,200	2,400	2,600	2,800	3,000	3,200
Fruits	1 cup	1 cup	1.5 cups	1.5 cups	1.5 cups	2 cups	2 cups	2 cups	2 cups	2.5 cups	2.5 cups	2.5 cups
Vegetables	1 cup	1.5 cups	1.5 cups	2 cups	2.5 cups	2.5 cups	3 cups	3 cups	3.5 cups	3.5 cups	4 cups	4 cups
Grains	3 oz-eq	4 oz-eq	5 oz-eq	5 oz-eq	6 oz-eq	6 oz-eq	7 oz-eq	8 oz-eq	9 oz-eq	10 oz-eq	10 oz-eq	10 oz-eq
Meat and Beans	2 oz-eq	3 oz-eq	4 oz-eq	5 oz-eq	5 oz-eq	5.5 oz-eq	6 oz-eq	6.5 oz-eq	6.5 oz-eq	7 oz-eq	7 oz-eq	7 oz-eq
Milk	2 cups	2 cups	2 cups	3 cups	3 cups	3 cups	3 cups	3 cups	3 cups	3 cups	3 cups	3 cups
Oils	3 tsp	4 tsp	4 tsp	5 tsp	5 tsp	6 tsp	6 tsp	7 tsp	8 tsp	8 tsp	10 tsp	11 tsp
Discretionary calorie allowance	165	171	171	132	195	267	290	362	410	426	512	648

United StatesDepartment of Agriculture Center for Nutrition Policy and Promotion April 2005 CNPP-XX

MyPyramid Food Intake Patterns

The suggested amounts of food to consume from the basic food groups, subgroups, and oils to meet recommended nutrient intakes at 12 different calorie levels. Nutrient and energy contributions from each group are calculated according to the nutrient-dense forms of foods in each group (e.g., lean meats and fat-free milk). The table also shows the discretionary calorie allowance that can be accommodated within each calorie level, in addition to the suggested amounts of nutrient-dense forms of foods in each group.

Vegetable Subgroup Amounts are Per Week												
Calorie Level	1,000	1,200	1,400	1,600	1,800	2,000	2,200	2,400	2,600	2,800	3,000	3,200
Dark green veg.	1 c/wk	1.5 c/wk	1.5 c/wk	2 c/wk	3 c/wk	3 c/wk	3 c/wk	3 c/wk	3 c/wk	3 c/wk	3 c/wk	3 c/wk
Orange veg.	.5 c/wk	1 c/wk	1 c/wk	.5 c/wk	2 c/wk	2 c/wk	2 c/wk	2 c/wk	2.5 c/wk	2.5 c/wk	2.5 c/wk	2.5 c/wk
Legumes	.5 c/wk	1 c/wk	1 c/wk	2.5 c/wk	3 c/wk	3 c/wk	3 c/wk	3 c/wk	3.5 c/wk	3.5 c/wk	3.5 c/wk	3.5 c/wk
Starchy veg.	1.5 c/wk	2.5 c/wk	2.5 c/wk	2.5 c/wk	3 c/wk	3 c/wk	6 c/wk	6 c/wk	7 c/wk	7 c/wk	9 c/wk	9 c/wk
Other veg.	3.5 c/wk	4.5 c/wk	4.5 c/wk	5.5 c/wk	6.5 c/wk	6.5 c/wk	7 c/wk	7 c/wk	8.5 c/wk	8.5 c/wk	10 c/wk	10 c/wk

United StatesDepartment of Agriculture Center for Nutrition Policy and Promotion April 2005 CNPP-XX

- Make notes on your dietary record as to how you compare to the daily requirements and portion sizes.

- It is important for your overall health to make the right food selections each day and also to make sure the portion sizes of the foods consumed are in line with the recommended daily requirements.

Portion Sizes

Being able to accurately estimate portion sizes according to the recommended MyPyramid is very important, but at the same time very confusing. Check out each section to find out the suggested amounts of food to consume from each group for your calorie level.

Are the portion sizes you are eating too large? Let's look and see. Start with the left side of the MyPyramid and work across to the right.

Grains: Many of the foods that belong in this section are carbohydrates. You know from Chapter 6 that carbohydrates are critical to our daily living.

The amount of Grains recommended each day is dependent on your calorie level as identified on the MyPyramid Food Intake Pattern chart. The recommendation for each calorie level is based on one-ounce equivalents (1 oz. eq). Listed on page 131 are a few examples of one-ounce equivalents for the Grains group.

One-ounce equivalents =

    1 slice bread

    1 cup of ready-to-eat cereal

    1/2 cup cooked rice, pasta or cooked cereal

    1 small flour or corn tortilla

    ~70-100 calories

Note: One-half of the Grain choices for the day should be from whole grain food choices.

In looking at the 2,000–calorie level on the MyPyramid Food Intake Pattern chart, six–ounce equivalents are recommended for the day, and three of these should be from whole grain foods. Choosing three whole grain foods is easily achieved. For example, two slices of whole wheat bread for a sandwich and one cup of whole grain cereal for breakfast. These tend to have a lower Glycemic Index, which is healthier.

- To determine if the food you have chosen is a whole grain, look at the ingredient list on the food label for the words "whole" or "whole grain." The grains will be listed as whole wheat, whole oats, whole rye and so on.

- Besides reaping the benefits of trace minerals from whole grains, the extra fiber helps to make you feel full and prevent constipation.

- If you are not accustomed to eating whole grains, gradually increase the amount consumed over several weeks to achieve your goal. This will avoid abdominal discomfort and allow your body to get used to the increase in whole grains in your daily diet.

- The carbohydrates in these foods help to quench hunger and make you feel satisfied.

How did your dietary record compare to the daily requirements from this food group? Too little or too much? Make a note
on your dietary record to see what changes you can possibly
make to improve your dietary intake from this food group.

The variety in this food group seems almost endless, which is
good. This means that we can make many more healthy choices.
Here are a few examples:

- Breads: bagels, English muffins, torti-
  llas, French, Italian, multi-grain, pita,
  pumpernickel, rye, sourdough, potato,
  white and whole wheat bread.

- Cereals: dry or cold unsweetened cereals, oatmeal, cream
  of wheat and grits.

- Pasta: spaghetti, elbow, penne, ziti, rigatoni, canneloni,
  lasagna, fettuccine, linguine, vermicelli, capellini, ravi-
  oli, couscous, egg noodles, and wonton wrappers. Pastas
  made with rice, whole wheat, corn, spinach, red bell pepper, buckwheat and beans.

- Rice: brown, white, wild, basmati, jasmine, texmati
  and wehani.

Vegetables: The next food group to the right
of Grains is Vegetables. Based on your daily caloric intake, check out your selected calorie level
on the MyPyramid Food Intake Pattern chart to
see how many vegetables are recommended each
day.   It may seem next to impossible to consume

that much. But actually, when you take a closer look, the goal is obtainable.

Remember that one of the problems contributing to obesity is that the portion size we serve is out of proportion to what we really need. We tend to consume way too much food! Vegetable portions are in the household measure of cups. Listed below are a few examples of what one cup is equivalent to for the Vegetable group:

One cup = 1 cup of raw or cooked vegetables
2 cups of raw, leafy vegetables
2 large celery stalks
1 medium potato
1 large pepper
1 large ear of corn
2 medium carrots
~25-300 calories

The Vegetable group recommendations are further divided into subgroups as shown on the Vegetable Subgroup Amounts Per Week chart on page 129. The subgroups of vegetables are dark green vegetables, orange vegetables, legumes (dried beans and peas), starchy vegetables, and other vegetables. Specific examples are given below for each subgroup:

- Dark green vegetables (fewer than 50 calories/1 cup vegetable equivalent): broccoli, collards, mustard greens, turnip greens, kale spinach, and raw, leafy vegetables like romaine, watercress, endive, escarole, and spinach

- Orange vegetables (~50-100 calories/1 cup vegetable equivalent): carrots, pumpkin, sweet potatoes, and acorn, butternut, and Hubbard squash

(Dark green and orange vegetables are rich sources of the antioxidant beta carotene.)

- Legumes (~200-300 calories/1 cup cooked): black beans, garbanzo beans (chickpeas), kidney beans, lentils, great northern beans, navy beans, pinto beans, soybeans, black-eyed peas (cowpeas), split peas, and tofu

- Starchy vegetables (~100-200 calories/1 cup cooked): corn, green peas, green lima beans, white potatoes

- Other vegetables (~30-70 calories/1 cup vegetable equivalent): asparagus, beans (wax and green), beets, brussels sprouts, cabbage, cauliflower, celery, cucumbers, leeks, lettuce, mushrooms, onions, okra, peppers (red, yellow, and green), squash (yellow and zucchini), and tomatoes

Again, look at the MyPyramid Food Intake Pattern to view the recommended amount of each subgroup per week for your caloric level. As you can see, there is great variation in the caloric content of vegetables, even when you don't consider other ingredients that may be used in cooking, like added fat or oil. All vegetables are good for eating; however, balancing the higher calorie choices with lower calorie choices within the same meal will help

Keep color in mind when selecting your veggies, especially those red, green and yellow ones. Besides being rich in nutrients, colorful vegetables can make your meal more appetizing! And don't forget, if kids see their parents enjoying vegetables, they are more likely to eat them, too.

to stay within your daily caloric allowance. For example, green peas, sweet potatoes, and corn within the same meal include a variety of color, texture, and nutrients, but they are all higher calorie choices. In order to meet your calorie level, broccoli, sweet potatoes, and yellow squash would provide the same variety of color and texture—and *fewer* calories—while still being rich in nutrients.

Don't let the higher caloric content of legumes keep you from including them in your diet. Legumes are rich in protein (without the fat found in meat), potassium, fiber, and many other nutrients. Their high soluble fiber level can help to lower blood cholesterol levels and control blood sugar levels when appropriately added to the diabetic diet. Since legumes may be used as a meat substitute, they can count in the meat or vegetable group. (One-fourth cup of cooked legumes can count as one-ounce meat equivalent.)

Remember to consume a minimum variety of vegetables for the week. For the 2,000–calorie level, three cups of dark green vegetables per week are recommended, along with two cups of orange vegetables, three cups of cooked legumes, three cups of starchy vegetables and six and one-half cups of other vegetables.

The variety of vegetables available seems almost limitless, which is good when trying to change to a healthier lifestyle. Surely there are some that you and your family can enjoy. The nutritional benefits are tremendous. They can provide fiber along with vitamins, minerals and antioxidants, which protect your body from many preventable diseases such as high blood pressure, high cholesterol, obesity and some cancers. Raw veggies also make great snacks and are low in calories.

Fruits: Moving along the MyPyramid from left to right, Fruits are next in line. When looking at the Food Intake Pattern chart for Fruits, you will see that the amount of Fruit recommended to be consumed each day is slightly less than for  Vegetables. The amount of recommended Fruit is measured in cups. Listed below are a few examples of the recommended portion sizes from the Fruit group:

One cup = 1 cup of chopped, fresh or
unsweetened canned fruit
1 cup (8 oz) of 100 percent fruit juice
1 large banana
1 large orange
½ cup of dried fruit
32 seedless grapes
~50-100 calories (except avocado;
1 medium avocado = ~300 calories)

A special recommendation for the Fruit group is to aim for less than half of the total fruit intake to come from juice. For the 2,000–calorie level, two cups of fruit are recommended for the day with less than one cup (8 ounces) from 100 percent fruit juice.

Think of eating fruits as nature's way of providing us with candy. These are great for meals and snacks. When you think about it that way, it's easy to get the amount you need each day.

1. Choosing unsweetened canned, frozen or dried fruit helps to decrease the amount of sugar eaten.

2. Selecting more fruit and less juice provides more fiber to your diet, which helps with satiety (fullness) and has the added benefit of cleaning the teeth!

3. Be sure to brush your teeth after eating dried fruit or eat it with other foods. Dried fruit tends to stick to the teeth and may cause tooth decay.

Using the list below, select a different fruit to eat each day.

Apples	Grapefruit	Pears
Applesauce	Grapes (green, red)	Pineapples
Apricots	Honeydew Melon	Plums
Bananas	Kiwi	Prunes
Blackberries	Oranges	Raisins
Cantaloupe	Mangos	Raspberries
Cherries	Nectarines	Strawberries
Dates	Papayas	Tangerines
Figs	Peaches	Watermelon

Did you make some notes on your dietary record about the fruits you are consuming or would like to consume?

 **Fats and Oils:** The next group on the MyPyramid is Fats and Oils. Including some fat and oil in your diet is necessary for good health. Dietary fats and oils are needed to help your body to absorb certain vitamins found in other foods and provide essential fatty acids needed in body functions and energy. Yes, too much fat in our diets can provide too much energy (calories). It's easy to get too much. Use the MyPyramid Food Intake Pattern chart to check the amount you need for your calorie level. Fats and oils are measured in teaspoons (tsp). Check out a few examples on page 138:

```
One teaspoon =   1 tsp of oil
                 1 tsp of margarine
                 1 tsp of mayonnaise
                 1 TB (tablespoon) of salad dressing
                 ~5 grams of fat
                 ~45 calories
```

The 2,000-calorie level from the MyPyramid Food Intake Pattern chart shows that the amount of oil recommended for daily consumption is six teaspoons.

When reading a food label, check out the grams of fat. This will give you an idea of how many grams of fat are found in one serving of the low fat or reduced fat food products like salad dressing, mayonnaise or margarine and how they would count toward the recommended amount. There are a few other foods that are primarily fat to watch for such as olives, avocados, nuts and seeds.

There is an emphasis on choosing fats that are mainly monosaturated and polysaturated rather than "solid fats" like saturated fat or trans fat (these have been discussed in Chapter 8). If "solid fats" are chosen, this is counted as part of your discretionary calories for the day. Discretionary calories will be discussed later in this chapter.

How well did you do for your Fat and Oil allowance for the day? Too much? What alternative choices could you have made to achieve your goal for the Fats and Oils group?

Milk, Yogurt, and Cheese: The next group after Fats and Oils on the MyPyramid is Milk. Using the MyPyramid Food Intake

Pattern chart, based on your daily calorie consumption, check to see how much Milk, Yogurt and Cheese you should be consuming each day. As you may notice, for all calorie levels, the recommended range for daily consumption is two to three  cups of milk each day. Keep in mind the recommended level is based on fat free (skim) or low fat (1 percent) milk or its equivalent of yogurt or cheese. (If you choose reduced fat or whole milk, yogurt or cheese, the difference in calories from fat free milk is counted in your discretionary calories allowance for each day.)

Milk products are measured in cups. Using a 2,000–calorie level from the MyPyramid Food Intake Pattern chart, the recommended amount for each day is three cups. Here are a few examples of what one cup is equivalent to:

> One cup = 1 cup milk or yogurt
> 1 ½ ounces of natural cheese
> 2 ounces of processed cheese
> ½ cup ricotta cheese
> 2 cups cottage cheese
> ~300 mg of calcium
> ~100 calories (except ½ cup ricotta cheese =
> ~170 calories and 2 cups cottage cheese
> = ~300 calories)

(Choices made should be fat-free or low fat products. The difference between whole milk choices and the low fat version counts as discretionary calories. Discretionary calories are discussed toward the end of the chapter.)

The foods in this group are sometimes referred to as dairy products. They are very important to our health. So look for these when you shop.

1. These foods are rich in protein, B vitamins, calcium and phosphorus.

2. Selecting the low fat versions will decrease the amount of saturated fat and calories.

3. Lactose free milk also helps those individuals with lactose intolerance.

4. And when you study the amount needed, it's really not that hard to get them in each day.

5. If you do not consume milk or milk products, consider including calcium-fortified products to meet your daily calcium needs. Check out the Nutrition Facts on the food label for this information.

How did your daily intake for this food group compare with the recommended amount for your calorie level from the MyPyramid Food Intake Pattern chart?

A Few Words about Milk and Weight Loss

Recent studies have found low fat dairy products in your daily diet helps with weight loss as long as the daily consumption is adequate. The exact reason why is undetermined.

Fat cells do store calcium. Calcium seems to play a role in how fat is stored and broken down. When the body has an adequate amount of calcium, particularly from low fat dairy products such as low fat milk and yogurt, weight loss is more significant. Also, fat seems to be lost more in the abdominal area. This is good news!

Does this mean you can eat anything you want and then drink a glass of skim milk and your body does not get fat? No. It simply means that getting enough calcium in the diet makes it easier for the body to get rid of fat. Does this mean that taking a calcium supplement could do the job instead of consuming low fat dairy products? Not completely. Even though taking a calcium supplement does help, the greatest benefit seems to be from the low fat dairy products.

The nutrient combination of protein, vitamins, and minerals found in dairy products may be the reason why. Most adult men need about 1,000 - 1,200 mg of calcium per day. Women need about 1,000 - 1,300 mg per day. If you opt for the supplement anyway, choose one with added vitamin D, zinc and magnesium to maximize calcium absorption by the body.

 **Meat, Poultry, Fish, Beans, Eggs, and Nuts:** The last major food group on the MyPyramid is Meat, Poultry, Fish, Beans, Eggs, and Nuts. This is sometimes referred to as the Meat and Beans group. The foods in this group high in protein and are very important in terms of growth and development. The importance of protein in the diet was discussed in Chapter 7.

Review the MyPyramid Food Intake Pattern chart to see how much meat you need to consume from this group each day. The recommended amounts are listed as ounce equivalents or oz. eq. For example, if your recommended calorie level is 2,000 calories a day, you would need to consume five and one-half ounce equivalents.

Listed are a few examples of what a one-ounce equivalent is equal to:

> One-ounce equivalents =
>> 1 oz. of meat, poultry or fish
>> ¼ cup of cooked meat
>> ¼ cup of cooked legumes (dried beans or peas)
>> 1 egg
>> 1 TB (tablespoon) peanut butter
>> ½ oz. nuts or seeds
>> ¼ cup tofu
>> ~50-100 calories

Usually it's not hard to get the recommended amount of food from this section. In fact this may be where you are getting too much. Look below and see what you think. Don't have a clue as to how much you are eating? Here are a few guidelines.

- 2 oz. meat equivalents = one chicken leg, one small hamburger patty, one ounce of nuts, two tablespoons of peanut butter or one-half cup of legumes

- 3 oz. meat equivalents = one average pork chop, one-half chicken breast, three-quarter cup of cooked meat, one and one-half ounces of nuts or three-quarter cup of cooked legumes

> **Baking, broiling, roasting, braising and grilling are the healthy choices of meat preparation.**

If you're really curious about how much meat you're eating, purchase a food scale and weigh the cooked meat. You will be surprised about how much you are consuming.

1. Note that the calories in one ounce of meat can range from 50 to 100, depending on the type and cut.

2. Maybe that 16-ounce steak is not really a good idea. Perhaps a 6-ounce cut is more in line with your daily needs.

3. Exceeding the amount of food for this group can stack up the excess calories in a hurry and cause the teeter-totter to tilt the wrong way! BEWARE! Also, remember those excess protein calories are converted into fat.

Lean meats are the way to go. Check it out below. Meats with five grams of fat or less in a 3-ounce portion are listed. These should be roasted, broiled, grilled or braised.

*Skinless Chicken Breast	Beef Top Round	Halibut
*Skinless Turkey Breast	Beef Tip Round	Orange Roughy
Pork Tenderloin	Cod	Shrimp
Beef Eye of Round	Flounder	

*Cooking with the skin on does not alter the calories significantly. However, not *eating* the skin is a leaner choice.

Before we move to the last group on MyPyramid, how did you do with the Meat group?

Discretionary Calorie Allowance: This is the last group on the MyPyramid. This is a new concept used by the MyPyramid in an attempt to quantify extra calories that you can use at your discretion. The amount of recommended extra calories can be found on the MyPyramid Food Intake Pattern chart. Your discretionary calories are separate from the food group calories. When calories are calculated for the various food groups, the calculation is based on foods that are fat free or low fat and have no sugar added. If you drink whole milk instead of fat free milk, the difference in calories counts toward your discretionary amount.

For example, at the 2,000-calorie level, the amount of discretionary calories that you have the option of eating is 267 calories. If you drink three cups of whole milk instead of fat free, you would use 240 of your discretionary calories. This would leave you only 27 calories for the balance of the day. How was this calculated?

- Three cups of whole milk is equivalent to 480 calories. One cup (8 oz) is equal to 160 calories (this information is on the food label). Three times 160 calories is 480 calories.

- Three cups of fat free milk is equivalent to 240 calories. One cup (8 oz) is equal to 80 calories. Three times 80 calories is 240 calories.

- The difference between 480 calories and 240 calories is 240. This is the amount of your discretionary calories used.

Choosing foods with less "solid" fat allows you to eat more and still stay within your calorie allowance for the day.

Look what happens to your discretionary calories when you consume just one 16-ounce regular soft drink. Upon reading the

food label, you discover your favorite 16-ounce soft drink has 200 calories from sugar. The sugar in the soft drink eats up 200 calories of your discretionary 267 calories. This would leave only 67 discretionary calories for the balance of the day.

Remember, in this example for a 2,000-calorie level day, those 267 discretionary calories are your total for the day and apply to any combination of sugar or solid fats consumed.

Your discretionary calories may be used by:

- Eating foods that contain mainly fat, sugars and/or alcohol like soda, wine or candy

- Adding extra fats and sugars to foods like jam, sugar, butter or sauces

- Choosing the higher "solid fats" or sugar form of a food such as whole milk, a pastry, sweetened cereal or yogurt

- Eating more than the recommended amounts from the main food groups

This is a new way of looking at how you use your calories. It is a bit cumbersome and even confusing. Think of your body as a calculator. Every bite of food or sip of beverage counts toward your daily calories consumed. Being smart about how you choose your foods each day is important. Each choice made each day can add to your good health or take away from it. Remember in Chapter 2, we discussed what body weight is all about. Achieving a healthy body weight is determined by calories consumed compared to calories burned. Calories do make the difference.

If you find that using the MyPyramid is just too complicated, consider this alternative. Choose a calorie level to meet your weight goal as discussed earlier. Compare your dietary record to the MyPyramid Food Intake Pattern chart for your chosen calorie level as a guide toward selecting a balanced diet from the basic food groups. This will ensure that you are getting the vitamins and minerals each day that are critical to your diet. If you eat something that is not on the MyPyramid or you don't know how it counts or where it fits, jot down the calories and keep these selections within

your allotted discretionary calorie allowance. You will be all right if you follow this alternative. Those food items that don't seem to fit anywhere are probably those extra items like pie, ice cream and cake. This next section is on snacking, which might help you make wiser selections that will impact how you choose to use your discretionary calories.

Snacks - where do these belong on the MyPyramid? You may be asking where the chips, candy, cookies and pies are. These food items are the ones that you should avoid or eat smaller portions, especially if you are trying to lose weight. Many of these foods contribute more to obesity, diabetes, heart disease and high blood pressure than any other foods. These foods are the things that should make up the least part of our daily diets.

Choose Snacks Wisely: Make the most (or least) of your snacking choices. **READ THE FOOD LABEL** so that you will know what you are eating. A few changes here can make a big difference. Look and see.

Simply choosing a healthier snack can result in significant changes in the calories you consume each day. The above comparison shows that choosing one medium blueberry bagel instead of

Your Snack	Alternative Snack	The Difference in Calories
4 chocolate chip cookies 240 calories	4 graham cracker squares 118 calories	122
1 cup ice cream 286 calories	1 cup fat free frozen yogurt 190 calories	96
4 cups buttered popcorn 140 calorics	2 cups buttered popcorn 70 calories	70
1 slice of apple pie 296 calories	2 fresh apples 162 calories	134
3 glazed doughnuts 726 calories	1 medium blueberry bagel 264 calories	462

Note: Food values obtained from <u>Bowes & Church's, Food Values of Portions Commonly Used,</u> 18th edition, Lippicott Williams and Wilkins

> A snacking suggestion is to make one healthy snack change for the home and one change for work.

three glazed doughnuts means you will consume 462 fewer calories. Let's say that on average you consume 200 fewer calories a day in snacks. This means over a period of one year you will consume 73,000 fewer calories. This adds up to a 21-pound weight loss for the year – a very good achievement. An additional benefit in choosing a healthier snack is that the alternative snack will probably have less saturated fat, trans fat and sugar.

Just making subtle changes in your snacking habits will result in positive lifestyle changes that will help you achieve your healthy body weight.

MyPyramid was developed by the U.S. Department of Agriculture.

Chapter 10:
A Final Word about Getting Started

The last few chapters discussed the importance of a balanced diet and how to achieve one. You read that consuming carbohydrates, protein and fat is the only way to achieve a balanced diet. More importantly, you read that by making subtle and simple changes in your diet without upsetting your "homeostasis," weight loss or controlling your body weight is achievable. However, the authors would be remiss if we did not comment on the diet craze. Knowledge regarding diets in terms of what is good and what is bad is critical in your decision to achieve a healthy body weight.

The Diet Craze

Going on an extreme fad diet and then off again results in a yo-yo effect on your body weight – you lose then you gain. Is this really good for you? Recently, a study reported that yo-yo dieting harms the immune system in women. If yo-yo dieting can cause harm to the immune system, what harm can it cause to other human systems such as cardiovascular, endocrine (hormones), digestive, nervous, muscular and renal (kidneys). Are you willing to take that chance? More and more studies are demonstrating that yo-yo dieting, while providing some short-term health benefits, may cause more harm than benefit to your health in the long-term.

Unfortunately, fad diets or quick fixes usually involve diets that are very unbalanced. Consider the following diets:

- Low carbohydrate, high fat
- High protein, high fat
- High carbohydrate, low protein
- Cabbage soup diet
- South Beach diet
- Atkins diet
- Scarsdale diet
- Three-Day diet
- Seven-Day, All You Can Eat diet
- Russian Air Force diet
- Grapefruit diet
- And the confusing list goes on

A Few Words about the Atkins Diet

The Atkins diet is an example of a diet craze that represents a controversy about overall health safety. This diet promotes

high protein and high fat foods and severely restricts carbohydrates. Restricting carbohydrates cuts the consumption of major food groups from the diet such as fruits, vegetables, breads and grain products, milk and yogurt, in addition to refined sugars found in soft drinks, fruit drinks, syrup, jelly, candy and so on. The brain's main source of energy is glucose, which is a carbohydrate. Glucose is more efficiently derived from carbohydrate food sources than protein and fat. Further, the Atkins diet deprives the body of critical essential vitamins, minerals, fiber and antioxidants found in carbohydrate foods. It is next to impossible to replace all of these with a single daily vitamin or supplement pill.

Because the Atkins diet is a high fat and high protein diet, there is concern that the consumption of these foods for the long-term places too much of a burden on body organs like the heart, liver and kidney. This can be harmful.

Would you lose weight with the Atkins diet plan? The answer is "probably." Would this diet cause you to miss dietary essentials? Absolutely. However, the most critical question, to which no one knows the answer, is will this diet harm you in the long-term?

The short-term effect of the Atkins diet has shown a decrease in triglycerides and an increase in HDL. This is a positive. However, it is the authors' opinion that a high protein, high fat diet for the long-term is not compatible with good health. There is too much restriction of the "good for you" foods.

So here is a suggestion: take the best from this extreme diet plan and use it. Eliminate those refined sugars. Without the sodas, doughnuts, cookies, candy, cake and pie, chances are you will lose weight, which will help lower your triglycerides and raise your HDL. But continue to eat  those carbohydrates that provide critical essential nutrients. A real benefit of this plan is that you can still enjoy the taste and nutritional benefits from whole grains, fruits, vegetables and low fat milk products. And in the long-term, you will probably minimize potential harm to your various body systems.

Every marketer is trying to convince you that their diet is the best for you! (Isn't it funny how everyone is watching out for you?) The authors' recommended approach is to provide facts for you about nutrition so you can make the decision as to what is best for you and your family!

Smart Shopping at the Supermarket

There are so many tempting foods available. As you stroll up and down the aisles of the local supermarket, be prepared and have a plan to keep you on track. Here are a few ideas.

- Make a list and stick with it. Plan meals for the coming week and make a grocery list of the food needed to prepare the meals. Maybe it is time to try a new recipe. Write down the items you need. It's a good idea to keep an ongoing list at home. Once you run low on staples, write them on the list. Keeping the pantry stocked will help the household run more smoothly.

- Check out the weekly sales ads. Seasonal fruits and vegetables are often cheaper in season and they have their best flavor...a double bonus! Take advantage of this. Stock up on food you can freeze anduse later. Just date them before you place them in the freezer so you can use them in a timely manner.

- Gather coupons that you've clipped from newspapers and magazines. Check out the grocery store website for coupons. Use coupons only for items you normally purchase or on an item you have been wishing to try. Compare prices at the store to determine if you are actually saving money.

- Experiment with store brands. Some store brand foods are actually produced by brand name companies. Store brands often save you money without compromising quality.

- Plan to shop when you are not hungry. You will buy less when you are not hungry and are more apt to stick to the grocery list.

- When in the store, check out the Nutrition Facts label if you are unsure about which products to buy.

Reading the Food Label

If you have never paid attention to the food label, maybe this is a good time to start. If you do read the food label, do you look at the calories, fat or sugar first? Well, back up a bit. All of the information on the food label is based on a serving size. First read what is a serving size for the food item selected.

Similar products may have different serving sizes depending upon the brand. The sample food label to the right shows the serving

Nutrition Facts
Serving Size 6 Crackers (28g)
Servings Per Container About 10

Amount Per Serving	
Calories 120	Calories from Fat 35

	% Daily Value*
Total Fat 4g	6%
Saturated Fat 0.5g	3%
Trans Fat 0g	
Polyunsaturated Fat 2g	
Monounsaturated Fat 1g	
Cholesterol 0mg	0%
Sodium 135mg	6%
Total Carbohydrate 20g	7%
Dietary Fiber 3g	13%
Sugars 0g	
Protein 3g	

Vitamin A 0%	•	Vitamin C 0%
Calcium 0 %	•	Iron 8%

*Percent Daily Values are based on a 2,000 calorie diet. Your daily values may be higher or lower depending on your calorie needs:

		Calories:	2,000	2,500
Total Fat	Less than		65g	80g
Sat Fat	Less than		20g	25g
Cholesterol	Less than		300mg	300mg
Sodium	Less than		2,400mg	2,400mg
Total Carbohydrate			300g	375g
Dietary Fiber			25g	30g

INGREDIENTS: WHOLE WHEAT, SOYBEAN OIL, MALTODEXTRIN, SALT, MONOGLYCERIDES, ROSEMARY, MONOSODIUM GLUTAMATE (FLAVOR ENHANCER), ONION POWDER, SPICES, OLIVE OIL, SPICE EXTRACTS, NATURAL FLAVOR.

size is 6 crackers. If you ate 12 crackers, multiply the numbers by 2. Twelve crackers would have 240 calories, 8 grams of fat, 6 grams of dietary fiber and so on.

There are totals for fat, cholesterol, sodium, carbohydrate and protein. Saturated fat, trans fat, polyunsaturated fat and mono-unsaturated fat are all parts of the total fat. Total carbohydrate is broken down into dietary fiber and sugars (which can be natural and/or added sugar).

And what do those percent numbers and Daily Value mean?

- Daily Value is based on a 2,000 calorie diet. The percent tells you what percentage of a nutrient is in a serving size relative to a 2,000 calorie diet.

- If no percent is given, then no recommendation has been established for that nutrient.

- A 5 percent Daily Value or less is considered low.

- A 20 percent Daily Value or more is considered high.

- With some nutrients, like vitamins, minerals or fiber, a high number is good.

- A high number for sodium, saturated fat or cholesterol is not considered healthy. Look for foods that have a low Daily Value for these nutrients.

- There is no percent Daily Value for trans fat. When comparing similar food products such as brands of marga-rines, add together the grams of the saturated fat and the trans fat. The lowest number for the total would be the best product if the serving sizes were the same for both.

 Though not a part of the Nutrition Facts, check out the ingredient list. This is particularly helpful in determining the types of oils that are used in a product and in whole grain products. Ingredients are listed in descending order according to the quantity of the item in the food. The ingredient listed first is the primary ingredient used in making the food and the ingredient listed last is the least.

So, you thought that brown bread you bought was whole grain? Check again. If whole grains were the tenth ingredient listed instead of the first, then there's not much whole grain in the bread. You were probably fooled by the color that was added to make it appear like whole grain bread.

And you say you never eat coconut oil? Check again. It may be in a food where you least expect it. If there is fat in the food, know the source – it will be listed in the ingredient list. It could be in your favorite hard candy or popcorn, or maybe in that delicious cake you buy at the store each week.

A little confused by sugar free, fat free, low sodium, cholesterol free and calorie free? There are a multitude of terms used that have been approved by the Food and Drug Administration (FDA).

- Just remember, sugar free does not mean that the food is also fat free and low in sodium.

- Often when something is eliminated, like sugar, then something else is increased to compensate for the flavor lost from sugar.

- A sugar free candy may be high in fat.

- A cereal that is low in sodium may be high in sugar.

If you are unsure about reading the totals for fat, calories, or sodium, then rely on the percent Daily Value. But remember, in general, **a 5 percent Daily Value or less is low and a 20 percent Daily Value or higher is high, based on one serving.**

Eating Out...the Healthy Way

If you enjoy eating out, make the most of it by choosing healthy foods. As obesity awareness increases and consumers demand healthier food choices, the selection of delicious, healthy foods should become easier to find. Many restaurants, including fast food places, are beginning to advertise  healthier alternatives. Take advantage of these new offers and try them when you're eating out.

If you frequently eat fast foods, ask for the nutrition information. This will allow you to study the restaurant offerings and compare the calorie and fat information, so you can make healthier selections. Most franchise-type establishments have this information on their websites. Check it out! Take time to write down what you normally eat and drink and then add up the calories and fat. Decide if you could make a better selection. Even a couple fewer calories will help keep off those extra pounds.

If you are visiting a new area or on vacation and plan to eat out, take a look at the menu posted outside the restaurant or check out the yellow pages in the phone book to see if the restaurant displays its menu in its ad. If possible, have a plan in mind as to the foods you want to eat and how you want them prepared before you order. If these options are not available, study the menu and before you order ask about the foods and how they are prepared.

Here are a few key terms, which usually indicate healthier options, to look for on the menu when ordering your meal. Try to select foods that are prepared the following way:

Asada	Baked	Blackened	Boiled
Broiled	Flame-cooked	Grilled	Light
Marinara	Marsala	Poached	Roasted
Simmered	Steamed	Vegetarian	Wine-based

Light, stir-fricd (ask about oil used)

Items on the menu prepared using the following terms should be avoided because they usually indicate high fat and high calorie foods:

Alfredo	Au gratin	Batter-dipped	Bearnaise
Bechamel	Breaded	Buttered	Crispy
Croquettes	Escalloped	Fried	Hollandaise
Mornay	Sautéed	Cream, creamed	or creamy

If you decide for a higher calorie choice, balance the meal with lower calorie items. For example, if you decide to have fried shrimp, then choose a fresh, garden salad with a fat free dressing, steamed vegetables, a roll without butter and a calorie-free beverage such as unsweetened iced tea or diet soda and skip the dessert.

When you are trying to lose weight, going to a restaurant when you are "absolutely starving" can be a mistake. When you feel really hungry, it's most likely that your blood sugar level has dropped, particularly if you have not eaten for over six hours. (This is a normal process that lets us know when we are hungry.)

■ Eating a small snack that contains 15-20 grams of carbohydrate 20 minutes before a meal can take the edge off hunger by raising the blood sugar level a small amount.

• This could be 1/2 cup (4 oz.) unsweetened juice, a medium piece of fruit, 1 slice of bread, or an 8 oz. glass of skim milk. The 60-80 calories from this small snack could literally shave off hundreds of calories in the restaurant.

• *This is a simple idea that can be used anytime when you have let yourself get too hungry.* If you are unable to do this, then choose a light appetizer such as vegetable juice or have a broth-based soup before your main entrée. Give it time to work (about 20 minutes) before you start the main course.

- Then eat until you are satisfied. Still have food left on your plate? Ask for a takeout container or leave it there. It's better to do this than to carry it home on your hips.

Here are some other healthful tips when eating out:

- Share an entrée or dessert with a friend who is with you.

- Order à la carte. Sometimes the portions are not as large.

- Steer away from food buffets. Buffets can add many calories quickly, especially when you are hungry simply because you eat too much.

- Ask for sauces and dressings on the side. This allows you to be the judge as to the amount used. Inquire about low calorie options in dressings, sauces and margarine.

- If you use sugar substitutes and have a favorite brand, carry a few packs with you. Sweetened beverages, particularly large sized or several refills, can add a couple hundred extra calories to your meal.

- Ask for a glass of water with your meal and drink it.

- If you visit a restaurant that has baskets of snack foods on the table as appetizers, such as corn chips, peanuts or breads, ask the server to remove them before you begin to consume them.

- Stretch the meal with conversation and relaxation. Sipping on a beverage and putting the fork down between bites allows you to recognize and feel that "just satisfied" feeling. This feeling is the signal to stop eating. Learn to recognize it and you will avoid that stuffed feeling after eating and all those extra calories.

If you eat out, you can still be healthy and lose weight, too. Each time you place an order, the choice is yours. Make it count and you will be on your way to achieving a healthy body weight.

No One Said Achieving a Healthy Body Weight Was Going to Be Easy!

How are you doing so far? Are you feeling overwhelmed by all the information you have been given? Well, if you are, that is normal. However, you now have at your fingertips all the information you need to create a balanced diet for you and your family. Now you can begin to assess where you need to make a change or two. Remember, you are going to start slowly so that the changes won't overwhelm you. Read on to get some ideas on how to pull it all together.

What kind of changes are you willing to make?

- Make healthier snacks available at home.
  - Offer more fruit, raw veggies and fruit juices instead of cookies and soft drinks. If possible, purchase the fruits and veggies already prepared and ready to eat.

- Prepare smaller portions at meal time.

- Pack a healthy lunch and take it to work instead of relying on the lunch special at your favorite diner or fast food restaurant – or even worse at the vending machines.

- When eating out:
  - Select smaller portions – stay away from the large and super-size portions.

  - Avoid restaurants that offer buffets. They may be faster than a restaurant but most people fill up on too much food. Even those salad bars are not as healthy as you may think if you put too much food on your plate. And, you must be aware of how much salad dressing you use. In other words, buffets are open–ended meals where the quantity of food is difficult to control because it is all so appealing.

- Start looking at the food labels on the foods you eat. Could you makc a better choice? Choose foods with less saturated fats and trans fats.

- Start asking for the nutrition information at fast food restaurants. Is there a food selection available that you could enjoy that has fewer calories and less fat?

- Bring a healthy snack from home for your mid-afternoon snack at work. Avoid the vending machines.

- Limit time in front of the TV and use the time for a family physical activity session.

Start Slowly

Just like getting involved with physical activity, you must walk before you run. The same is true with changes to your nutritional habits. You have been eating and preparing food, your way, for years. You are accustomed to certain meats, snacks and drinks. So the changes you make should be gradual – done slowly over a period of time.

As you make changes in the food you prepare, the food you purchase and the snacks you choose, write them down and post them on the refrigerator as a constant reminder of the positive changes you are making for yourself and your family.

We hope, based on what you have read so far, you have decided to take control of your health. This is a big decision – a big decision that can impact your life and your family members. Now is the time to get the whole family involved. Talk it over with everyone and together decide what you can do to improve your eating habits. If everyone understands what is at stake, getting them on board will be easier. But remember, if your family includes young children, you are in charge. You are responsible for their health, as well as your own. And the changes you make now could be the difference between a lifetime of productivity and well-being or a lifetime of out-of-control body weight and related medical problems.

Remember, it is the combination of smart eating and physical activity that will make it possible for you to achieve a healthy body weight.

Highlights – Healthy Eating Section

You now have completed reading the section on nutrition and healthy eating. To make sure you understand the critical components of body weight management and nutrition, we have highlighted several points that should be the focus of your program to achieve a healthy body weight. Following each statement is the page number where you can find additional information.

1. The body likes "homeostasis" – to be in balance. The body does not like extreme or radical changes. Changing your diet too quickly is extreme. Fad diets are extreme. You lose weight quickly by eliminating essential food groups or by adding certain foods. Extreme changes are not healthy for your body.
   Page 77

2. The body is very complex. Every day thousands and thousands of chemical reactions take place in the body. These are very normal reactions, but most importantly, they are extremely critical to our everyday bodily functions.
   Page 77

3. The smart approach is to monitor the calories eaten each day and to make sure the calories come from a balanced diet.
   Page 79

4. Carbohydrates and fat are the primary sources of energy. Protein can supply energy but its main function is for the growth and maintenance of body tissue.
   Page 79

5. Fiber is another type of carbohydrate. It is an indigestible substance found in certain foods. Fiber has been in and out of the news for the last ten years because it lowers blood cholesterol and possibly protects against colon cancer.
Page 86

6. If you are interested in losing weight, work to include some high fiber foods in meals and snacks because they help to fill you up and in most cases are low in calories.
Page 87

7. What is the Glycemic Index? It is the rate at which the body converts carbohydrates into blood sugar and how high the blood sugar climbs. For example, white bread is digested almost immediately into glucose causing the blood sugar to rise quickly. So white bread would have a high GI. On the other hand, milk or legumes take longer to digest, causing the blood sugar to rise more gradually, and therefore have a lower GI rating. In terms of the body and its response to blood sugar levels, it is healthier to have blood sugar levels rise gradually than to spike quickly.
Pages 90 - 91

8. Protein is made of components called amino acids. There are 22 amino acids identified in the body. Nine of these are referred to as "essential amino acids." The reason for this is that they are not produced by our bodies and must come from our diets.
Page 95

9. Imagine what would happen to your body weight simply by consuming smaller portions each day. The net result would be significant weight loss – a good and smart way to achieve a healthy body weight.
    Page 100

10. Fat is a concentrated energy source and is essential to our bodies. We need a minimum of 25-35 grams of fat each day. Fat is used for the absorption of the fat-soluble vitamins A, D, E and K. Caution: With no fat in the diet, these vitamins are not absorbed.
    Page 103

11. Saturated fats raise blood cholesterol levels and LDL (low density lipoproteins). Whenever possible, foods that contain saturated fats should be avoided. Monounsaturated fats may help lower LDL. Fats that contain monounsaturated oils are healthier for you. Polyunsaturated fats tend to lower LDL but too much of them can also decrease HDL (high density lipo-protein).
    Pages 104 - 105

12. Avoiding trans fatty acids could be one of the best things you can do for your health. By eliminating trans fatty acids from your diet, you are limiting LDL (bad cholesterol) and many extra calories. Because of this, many people are also able to shave away a few extra pounds just by avoiding foods that contain trans fats.
    Page 116

13. The best way to know where to start in terms of your nutrition is by taking a good look at what you and your family are actually eating. It involves writing and recording all the food consumed over a three-day period. This is called a dietary record. If you find keeping a dietary record for three days is impossible, at least keep a record for one typical day. **Pages 121 - 122**

14. Recent studies have found low fat dairy products in your daily diet helps with weight loss as long as the daily consumption is adequate. The nutrient combination of protein, vitamins and minerals found in dairy products may be the reason why. Most adult men need about 1,000 – 1,200 mg of calcium per day. Women need about 1,000 – 1,300 mg per day. **Pages 140 - 141**

15. Baking, broiling, roasting, braising and grilling are the healthy choices of meat preparation. **Page 143**

16. Simply choosing a healthier snack can result in significant changes in the calories you consume each day. Just making subtle changes in your snacking habits will result in positive lifestyle changes that will help you achieve your healthy body weight. **Pages 147 - 148**

17. Going on an extreme fad diet and then off again results in a yo-yo effect on your body weight – you lose then you gain. Is this really good for you? Recently, a study reported that yo-yo dieting harms

the immune system in women. If yo-yo dieting can cause harm to the immune system, what harm can it cause to other human systems such as cardiovascular, endocrine (hormones), digestive, nervous, muscular and renal (kidneys). Are you willing to take that chance?

Page 149

18. If you enjoy eating out, make the most of it by choosing healthy foods.
Page 156

19. When you are trying to lose weight, going to a restaurant when you are "absolutely starving" can be a mistake.
Page 158

20. Just like getting involved with physical activity, you must walk before you run. The same is true with changes to your nutritional habits. You have been eating and preparing food, your way, for years. You are accustomed to certain meats, snacks and drinks. So the changes you make should be gradual – done slowly over a period of time.
Page 162

Section Three

The Heart "E" Heart Approach to a Healthy Lifestyle for Children and Their Parents

Chapter 11:
Why Heart "E" Heart?

More of our children will be exposed to a lifetime of obesity and diabetes than any other generation of children in the history of our country. The impact of this on their health as they become adults will result in a very serious medical and economic burden on them and to our society. Teaching pre-school age children and primary grade children how to become more physically active and eat nutritiously is critical to abolishing this epidemic!

The probability of your children becoming physically disabled or chronically ill because of obesity at an early adult age is greater now than at any other time in American history. No parents wish this on their children. You can prevent this from occurring by making changes to promote healthy lifestyle habits for your children at a very young age.

The research the authors conducted in the 1970s clearly showed that children could not be forced to become more physically active or eat more nutritiously. The research supported an old cliché – "you can lead a horse to water but you can't make it drink." But when an educational program was introduced to teach primary grade children why they should become more physically active and eat nutritiously, they did. So the authors knew then that if the right education program were put forth, children would make the appropriate lifestyle behavior changes. The authors also learned that as the children were becoming more physically active and eating more nutritiously, so did their parents.

Remember, for the most part when your children are in school, school is a **sedentary** activity. Children spend much of their time during the day sitting at their desks. By the end of the day, they are raring to go. They need the time to blow off steam when they get home. Provide your children the opportunity to play, climb, run and have fun. They will benefit from the activity and so will you.

What can be done to reduce the seriousness of the health risks facing our children and to enhance the health and well-being of our families?

Education Is the Key!

It is time to teach children how to take better care of themselves – to become more physically active, eat nutritiously, be safe and avoid tobacco and drugs. Programs are needed that enhance the health and well-being of young children.

Children are inundated with food commercials that appear on TV. The average American child sees 10,000 food commercials a year on TV according to Kelly Brownell, a Yale University professor. About 95 percent of these commercials are for sugar packed or high fat foods. In 1998, two-thirds of the 11,000 new food products that appeared on the grocery shelves were loaded with fat or sugar. Add to this the impact of the fast food industry - *we are literally super-sizing ourselves to death!* Although the fast food industry and food manufacturers are trying to make healthier options available to the public, a lot more still needs to be done.

It is very difficult for parents or schools to compete with that amount of advertising. Physical education classes have disappeared from elementary schools and at the same time our school cafeterias have become fast food havens. (Parents need to become more active in their children's schools to make sure that physical education and recess, as well as more nutritious lunches and snacks, are part of their children's school day). No wonder there are so many obese, diabetic and inactive children.

Although many feel that classroom teachers, health educators and physical educators can make a significant difference in reversing this terrible trend of increased obesity and diabetes among children, parents should play an even greater role. Parents need to be more involved in promoting the health and well-being of their children. It may mean making unpopular decisions, such as turning off the TV. However, decisions that may be difficult in the short run can be very beneficial in the long run.

With this in mind, we want to introduce you to Heart "E" Heart to help your children achieve a healthy lifestyle early on and reverse the disturbing health trend of obesity and diabetes.

 Heart "E" Heart was developed to deal with very serious but preventable lifestyle disorders (obesity and diabetes) in such a way that everyone can learn why and what needs to be done to improve their health. Heart "E" Heart and his cast of friends delve into serious health issues that impact everyone.

Heart "E" Heart's concepts encompass all age groups – from infants to senior citizens. Heart "E" Heart's approach to a healthy lifestyle is easy to learn and it stays with you. It is entertaining so that all family members can enjoy it while making subtle changes in your lifestyle that will become permanent.

Heart "E" Heart was developed to teach healthier lifestyle habits in a simple, fun and achievable manner.

Losing weight, whether for a child or adult and becoming more physically fit takes time and it must be kept simple. Overloading a child, or even an adult, with too many things to keep track of in terms of what to eat and what activities to do, becomes a burden and soon the program falls by the wayside. The Heart "E" Heart approach does take time but he does keep it simple.

Let Us Meet Heart "E" Heart and Friends.

 Heart "E" Heart: This character sets the gold standard for a positive lifestyle to include vigorous physical activity, good nutrition and avoidance of drugs, alcohol and tobacco. Everyone wants to be like Heart "E" Heart. He is a lovable, compassion-

ate character who will be a friend to all – healthy and unhealthy. **Heart "E" Heart** is always safe. When it comes to teaching your child about safety, **Heart "E" Heart** is a good role model. Not only does **Heart "E" Heart** use all the appropriate safety gear when exercising (such as wearing his helmet when riding his bike), but he also practices safe habits by avoiding strangers, fire (matches), poisons and so on.

Lazy Heart: He doesn't exercise much and always takes the easy way out. Lazy Heart is a lovable character who just needs an extra push when it comes to exercise and nutrition. **Heart "E" Heart** is always willing to help Lazy Heart become a healthy character.

Smoker Heart: Smoker Heart has a bad habit—he smokes! The smoke pollutes his blood and creates the purplish color seen  in the illustration. Smoker Heart also doesn't pump blood as well as **Heart "E" Heart** and therefore finds it difficult to exercise. **Heart "E" Heart** is very willing to help Smoker Heart quit so he too can become healthy.

Fit Fat Cell: Everyone has fat cells—millions of them. Fit Fat Cell stays healthy by exercising and eating low fat and unsweetened foods. Fit Fat Cell has a small amount of Thundering Triglycerides. He is a fun character with lots of energy!

Bulgy Fat Cell: Unfortunately, when Fit Fat Cell doesn't exercise and eats too much, especially foods with lots of fat and

sugar, he becomes a Bulgy Fat Cell. He also has many more Thundering Triglycerides than Fit Fat Cell. Bulgy is an unhappy character with very little energy. He prefers to lie about watching TV and videos.

Thundering Triglyceride: Thundering Triglyceride is basically very good. He is a good energy source. But if we accumulate too many Thundering Triglycerides from lack of exercise and too much fat, sugar and alcohol, they will make Fit Fat Cell become Bulgy Fat Cell. This can lead to high blood pressure

and other kinds of diseases. Thundering Triglyceride is a strong character who always strives to be healthy.

Tidy Lipid: Tidy Lipid is another healthy lifestyle character. He works hard to keep the blood vessels clean so blood full of

rich nutrients can flow to all parts of the body. Physical activity and good nutrition make even more Tidy Lipids. Tidy Lipid is a charming char- acter, always ready to take part in **Heart "E" Heart** activities and healthy meals.

Sticky Lipid: Sticky Lipid doesn't know much about exercise and good nutrition. His lack of exercise and

diet high in fatty foods clogs the blood vessels, which will block the flow of blood to other parts of the body. Over time this can cause some very serious diseases. Although Sticky Lipid is a grouchy character, with a little bit of prodding from Heart "E" Heart and Tidy Lipid, he is ready to change his lifestyle habits.

Healthy Blood Pressure: We all need blood pressure to make sure the rich nutrients reach all parts of the body. The walls of the blood vessels, however, can tolerate only so much pressure. Healthy Blood Pressure is careful to exercise and eat properly, especially avoiding sodium, to keep the pressure from becoming too high. He is an optimistic character, ready to help the unhealthy characters become healthy.

Risky Blood Pressure: When we don't exercise and eat foods high in sodium and other poor nutritious foods, we run the risk of raising our blood pressure. If the pressure becomes too high, the walls of the blood vessels could weaken and burst. Risky Blood Pressure is caused by too many Bulgy Fat Cells, Thundering Triglycerides and a Lazy Heart. Risky is a grumpy, stressed out character not quite sure how to become healthy.

Well, now you have met **Heart "E" Heart** and his friends! One of the unique aspects of the **Heart "E" Heart** program is how the characters interact and interrelate to each other. Here is one example: too many Thundering Triglycerides will make a Fit Fat Cell become a Bulgy Fat Cell, which can turn a Healthy Blood Pressure into a Risky Blood Pressure. You and your children will learn that a lifestyle decision could have a "snowball" effect on your health – either good or bad.

Soon you will be able to relate many lifestyle hab
"E" Heart and his friends.   You will learn about different Heart
"E" Heart activities. When an activity is identified as a Heart
"E" Heart activity, you will know that it is good and healthy for
you and your family. **Foods identified as Tidy Lipid, Fit Fat Cell
or Healthy Blood Pressure foods are healthy for you.** Foods that
**should be avoided or limited are Sticky Lipid, Bulgy Fat Cell or
Risky Blood Pressure foods.**

Heart "E" Heart provides a win-win situation for everyone!
Your children, with your support and guidance, will become
more physically active and eat more nutritiously.   Children naturally want to be healthy – they don't like being sick.

Because Heart "E" Heart presents healthy lifestyle topics in
a fun, entertaining and non-threatening way, your children will
embrace the Heart "E" Heart program. And so will you! Your
children can and will make better decisions to promote a positive,
healthy lifestyle. And it all starts in the home! Mom and Dad need
to set Heart "E" Heart examples for their children to follow. That
is why the attached Heart "E" Heart program is not just for the
children, but for the entire family. Even grandparents can learn
from Heart "E" Heart.

Chapter 12:
Let Children Be Children!

Children are born to be physically active. Children like to be active, to run and play games - it is all very natural for them. Then why is there so much obesity and diabetes among our children due to the lack of physical activity?

There are Many Reasons for This:

- Some people say that it is because it is too dangerous to have our children play alone outside on the streets - it is not safe without parental supervision.

- Others say that it is because of working parents or single parents. As a result, the parents have less time to "play" with their children. Some experts blame competition. Placing very young children into organized sports takes away from their exploratory nature of just playing. Children, at a very early age, are forced to become very structured and organized. They lose the ability to just play and be creative with play by making up games that fit them and their needs. They lose interest in physical activity.

- Some say it is TV and computer games - Lazy Heart activities. Children spend too much time in front of the TV or computer monitor - and not enough time playing, either inside or outside.

- And finally, some say that kids eat way too much in their early childhood. They get exposed to "junk" food way

179

too soon – Sticky Lipid, Bulgy Fat Cell and Risky Blood Pressure foods.

Unfortunately, if the problem were just one of the above reasons, the fix would be fairly easy. But if your children are not physically active and/or obese, it is probably due to more than one of the above reasons.

Safety

No matter what you do to promote a Heart "E" Heart healthy lifestyle with your children, you *never* want to compromise your children's safety. Making a child go out and play in an area that is not safe is wrong. But at the same time, it is not an excuse to deny your children an opportunity to play. You need to be creative to find ways to provide your children an opportunity to play. It might mean creating play activities in the home, taking your children to a playground, or joining a YMCA or some other community group that provides play opportunities. Take advantage of your tax dollars at work. Play is a wonderful way to promote a Heart "E" Heart.

Getting involved with promoting a physically active lifestyle for your children may mean that you need to make sacrifices, specifically some of your time. But we feel very strongly that the sacrifices you make for your children far outweigh the potential health problem your children may face without a physically active lifestyle. Oh yes, Heart "E" Heart wants us to remind you that you might benefit from the activity too!

Take the time to discuss safety with your children. The safety concerns related to physical activity discussed on pages 31 - 34 for adults also apply to children. Set a good example when exercising by using the appropriate protective gear and practicing good safety habits. Your children will follow and learn from your example.

Don't be foolish when it comes to cold weather with your children. Being outdoors in the cold can be fun and healthy. But it is not too smart to go outdoors to play in extreme cold (when the temperatures are in the teens and the wind chill is in the single digits). Under these conditions, offer physical activity ideas that your children can do indoors, until the extreme cold passes.

Make sure your children drink plenty of water each day. If your children are active (and we hope they are), encourage them to drink plenty of water, fruit juices (not fruit drinks) and low fat milk. Children perspire and can lose a good proportion of their body fluid rather quickly (much faster than an adult). This can cause them to become dehydrated much faster than an adult, which can be very dangerous!

Play

A very simple word - play. But unfortunately, our young children are not given many opportunities to just play. Organized sports have contributed greatly to the loss of play activities. Organized sports used to be for children starting around age ten. Now parents can enroll their children in some sports as young as three years. Can you imagine that – a toddler playing organized sports!

Why do parents do this? In some cases, it is for very good reasons – child development, skill development, fitness development and social development – all very important in developing a Heart "E" Heart. But in most cases, it doesn't just stop there. It is to begin to train their children so they can become Olympic athletes or college athletes with scholarships! What started out as a good premise went by the wayside. The probability of a three-year-old child becoming an Olympic athlete is so remote that it doesn't even come close to justifying putting your children through the agonies of devoting their entire childhood to learning one sport. Their ability to learn how to be creative with play is lost at a very early age. This could have a negative impact on their attitude toward physical activity later in life when it is extremely critical.

Young children who are placed into regimented programs more than likely could end up being turned off to physical activity at an older age because of a bad experience. It is a bit ironic that in some cases too much regimented physical activity in the early years can lead to a Lazy Heart in later years. This is the exact opposite of what Heart "E" Heart is trying to accomplish.

Heart "E" Heart encourages parents to let children play and to join programs to promote play and child development with no competition until after the age of eight years. Give your children a chance to learn how to play and to grow physically and emotionally without the risk of injury - either socially or physically.

TV

Certainly our children are exposed to too much TV - a Lazy Heart activity. At a very early age the TV becomes a babysitter - put in a video or DVD and your children will watch it. Children develop a bad habit early, but not by their choice; it's the choice of mom or dad. Some educational TV programs are good for infants and toddlers. Some programs now encourage young children to do exercises while watching TV.

But the best thing to do to create good, healthy habits at an early age is to limit TV watching to one hour a day. If you extend the time, then make sure your children do some sort of physical activity either during the TV watching or some other time during the day.

Unfortunately, what goes along with TV watching is eating. This usually involves unhealthy snacks - those Sticky Lipids and Risky Blood Pressure foods such as cookies, chips and soda. Limit the number and kinds of snacks made available from the onset when your children watch TV. This will begin to create a healthier

behavior if your children know that if they elect to snack while watching TV, the snack will be small in size and healthy (such as raw veggies, fruit, whole wheat crackers). Snacks like these will promote Fit Fat Cells and Healthy Blood Pressure. Also, unscheduled snacking interferes with eating at meal times. The main problem with snacking is that children begin to associate watching TV with snacking. They snack out of habit, not because they are hungry. Heart "E" Heart discourages this kind of activity.

Computer Games

Computer games have a place in the developing child's lifestyle. It is not uncommon today to see four- and five-year-olds using a computer. There is an abundance of very good educational software for toddlers and young school age children.

Heart "E" Heart encourages parents to select software for toddlers and primary grade children that is educational and interactive. Heart "E" Heart discourages parents from purchasing games that have any kind of violence.

Again, like TV watching, the time spent playing computer games should be limited and not be used to replace the child's normal play time.

The computer should never be placed in a child's room where there is no or limited supervision. Place it where the computer can be used as a family event. That also allows mom or dad to make sure no bad habits are developing associated with the computer.

Like while watching TV, limit the kinds of snacks and the portion sizes your children may eat to Heart "E" Heart snacks while using the computer.

A Child Is Not an Adult

Everything about a child is smaller than an adult. When walking, a parent takes one step and a child may need to take three steps just to keep up.

In many instances, a child does not become fully developed physically until late in his or her teens. The most critical time of development occurs within the first eight years of a child's life. That is why this book is focusing only on infants through primary grade children.

Many lifestyle habits and behaviors are established by the time a child is eight. This means physical activity habits and eating habits are pretty well set and are very difficult to change after the age of eight!

This is not a book on child development but we need to mention a few items that are critical in order to protect the developing child from too much physical activity or food.

- Physical Development: A child's physical development limits the kinds of physical activities that he or she can do.

185

- Their lungs are still developing, which limits their ability to play or compete at the same level as older children and adults. A one-mile walk for a parent may seem easy, but to a child it is like walking five miles.

- The nervous system takes a long time to develop. This is why teaching young children basic skill development such as walking, hopping, jumping, climbing, catching and throwing at a very early age are important. It is fun for children to learn these skills and these **Heart "E" Heart** skills can be taught right in your own home. Teaching them also provides good family time together.

- A child's bones don't fully harden until early teenage years. When a child is first born, most of his or her bones are in the form of cartilage.  Over time the bones begin to harden (calcify), but until then a child is very prone to damage to their bones. Children's bones have growth plates. In the long thigh bone (femur), there are two growth plates – one at either end. Growth plates can become inflamed and in some instances damaged, to a point where it will stunt the child's growth – caused by too much repeated intense physical activity. This is one reason why organized sports that promote competition instead of skill development can be harmful. The repetitiveness of the practices and games becomes detrimental to the child's normal growth and development. Sports that have a body weight requirement

or implied requirement (wrestling, gymnastics) are
extremely dangerous to a young child's growth.

• Another system parents sometimes ignore is the
digestive system. A child's digestive system continues
to develop for many years after birth. This is why
Heart "E" Heart is careful not only in terms of the
food he recommends, but also in the size of the portion. Too many times a parent puts too much food
on a child's plate. It is not possible then for a child to
eat everything and then this becomes a contentious
moment. No one wins here – neither the parent
nor the child. Chapter 13 has further discussion
on this matter.

By now we hope you get the picture that a child is not an
adult. We must always remember this when we begin to encourage children and lead them down a path of a Heart "E" Heart
healthy lifestyle.

Let the Fun Begin!

As a parent, you can turn physical activity
and healthy eating into fun Heart "E" Heart
events for your children.

■ For infants, encourage movement by gently moving their
arms and legs. Move the arms overhead, out to the side,
across the body, up and down and in circulating movements. Move the legs back and forth and gently in circulating motions. These kinds of movement patterns help

to develop your child's neuromuscular system. Limit the amount of time an infant spends strapped in an infant seat. This restricts movement.

- After children can sit up, get down on the floor and "play" with them. Turn the music on and play and move to the music. (Yes, it is okay to dance.) Roll a ball to them (select a ball size that they can handle). Use building blocks and build them small things that a child can replicate. This helps children develop hand-eye coordination. Help children play with their toys.

- As children begin to walk, get them out of the stroller and let them walk and continue to encourage movement activities.

- As your child begins to talk or understand you, ask your child what kind of activities he or she wants to do. Listen to him or her. You would be surprised by what he or she might say or choose. Be venturesome with your child. Try what he or she wants to do. Afterall, you already had your chance to be a child; now it is time for your child.

- As your child begins to eat whole foods, offer your child a variety of healthy snacks. By introducing a variety of foods early, your child will be more willing to explore eating them. But always consider your child's safety when selecting snacks (see Chapter 13).

As stated repeatedly throughout this book, always be safe when it comes to physical activity and eating. Make sure the toys your children play with fit them. Watch for small pieces or pieces that can easily break off and cause a child to choke. Be careful that the foods you feed your children can be safely swallowed.

Use Heart "E" Heart to get your children moving or snacking on healthy foods. Include Heart "E" Heart in daily discussions: "Let's go to the store to buy some Heart 'E' Heart foods," or "Let's go do a Heart 'E' Heart physical activity!" When your children are watching too much TV, ask them if Heart "E" Heart would be watching TV or if he would be playing. Or if your children ask for a cookie for a snack, remind them that Heart "E" Heart would probably snack on an apple or carrot stick. As your children learn more about Heart "E" Heart , they will begin to make healthier choices without too much prodding from you.

A Quick Review on How to Get Started with an Exercise Program:

- To keep your children's hearts healthy like Heart "E" Heart, your children must engage in vigorous activities.

- These activities include but are not limited to:

Jogging	Swimming	Bicycling	Jumping Rope
Skating	Aerobics	Dancing	Rollerblading
Soccer	Walking	Floor Hockey	Self–Defense

- Children should engage in activities that elevate the heart rate to a range of 150 -160 beats per minute or higher for *at least 30 minutes every day of the week.*

- Children should participate in a variety of physical activities – not just cardiovascular or aerobic kinds of activities. Muscular strength is also very important, especially for the upper body.  Developing strong arms and shoulders at a young age will help protect the shoulder joint as children become older. This is particularly important for females. Activities that involve climbing, hanging and supporting the upper body with the arms will help develop strong shoulders.

- You can make physical activity a part of your children's everyday life by setting the right example: take the stairs rather than the elevator; walk to a nearby store rather than drive; use a push lawnmower rather than a riding mower.

- It is unhealthy to choose mainly Lazy Heart activities that avoid physical activity like:

  - watching television
  - sitting during recess
  - playing video games
  - playing with the computer

Should Children Lift Weights?

The good news is that recent research clearly shows that children (both boys and girls) can benefit from weightlifting activities. There are two primary concerns that must be strictly enforced when allowing your children to weightlift.

First, children should not be exposed to lifting heavy weights. The weight to be lifted should allow your children to perform at least 15 repetitions and up to 20 repetitions. Even when finishing the 20th repetition, the weight should not be so heavy that your children can not lift it. *The key is no straining.* Heavy weights could cause harm to a child's young body, especially the bones.

Second is safety. Most fitness facilities will not allow children to use the strength machines and this is good. The strength machines in a fitness facility are made to accommodate the anatomy of an adult – not a child – which creates a safety issue. Very few strength machine manufacturers make machines to fit children. This means that if you want your children to lift weights, they must rely on free weights – dumbbells and barbells. The concern is selecting a weight that a child can control at all times. A weight too heavy may cause the child to lose his or her balance and drop the weight. *So adult supervision is absolutely critical when your children are lifting weights.*

It is okay to expose children as young as eight years to weightlifting activities. Younger children can get involved with alternative weightlifting experiences. They could use stretch/elastic bands or light-weighted balls. They could also do the same strengthening exercises you do with cans in a plastic bag. The weight can be easily adjusted for your children. Children love to emulate their mom or dad – you could make that a family activity. And don't forget, children love to go to the playground. There are many upper body strengthening activities that your children can do at the playground such as climbing on the monkey bars. Activities such as biking, rollerblading and hiking are good strengthening exercises for your children's leg muscles.

Chapter 13:

Make Meals a Family Affair!

The most important challenge for parents, in developing healthy eating habits for their children, is to set a good example. Children learn to like the foods they see their parents eating and enjoying. A key to obtaining this goal is to have healthy foods available that taste good. As you introduce healthy foods to your children, refer to them as **Heart "E" Heart** foods. As your children come to learn more about **Heart "E" Heart**, they will make the right choice and choose **Heart "E" Heart** foods instead of Sticky Lipid, Bulgy Fat Cell or Risky Blood Pressure foods. And guess what, by setting a good **Heart "E" Heart** example, this will also mean better and healthier choices for you!

Remember, the foods available to your children are primarily under your control while they are small. After all, they can't drive to the nearby store to purchase their desires. It is a good idea to take a quick inventory of what's in your home. If the cupboards, refrigerator and freezer are full of high fat (Sticky Lipid), high salt (Risky Blood Pressure) and high sugar foods (Bulgy Fat Cells), then it is time to make a change. Begin to purchase more **Heart "E" Heart**, Fit Fat Cell and Healthy Blood Pressure foods such as fresh fruit, veggies, poultry and fish. A more detailed list will be provided later on in this chapter.

Introducing a New Food

Don't be afraid to introduce new foods to the family. When doing so, make positive comments about trying a new food and on its good taste, especially if it is a Heart "E" Heart food. Let your child know that this is the kind of food that Heart "E" Heart would eat. This is a much wiser and smarter approach than forcing or coercing a child to eat the new food. Repeated exposure to this new food will make the food more familiar and increase the likelihood of the child trying it. Bribing or pleading for a child to eat the food gives the child control, which he or she will realize quickly and then take advantage of the situation.

Keep Food Choices Simple

Most children enjoy plain foods rather than combination foods as in casseroles. Keep the prepared foods you offer your children simple. They also prefer that their foods not be heavily seasoned or served with gravies and sauces. This actually makes meal

 planning and food preparation easier for you. More importantly, by eliminating gravies and sauces, you are eliminating many extra calories and in some instances removing Sticky Lipid and Risky Blood Pressure foods from the meal – these are good and positive Heart "E" Heart changes!

How Much Food Do Children Need?

Often parents become concerned about their children's nutrition and wonder if they are getting what they need. Rest assured that if they are being offered a wide variety of healthy, nutritious foods at meals and for snacks, they are. Something to keep in mind is that children's portions should be smaller than adults'. Except for milk, children need the same number of servings from each of the food groups identified in Chapter 9 as adults, but in smaller amounts.

Keep in mind that your children's nutritional needs are high but their stomachs are small. Serve small portions and offer a variety of **Heart "E" Heart** healthy foods. If your children are hungry, then allow second portions. Their appetites vary. It is normal for your children to eat more at certain times and then cut back at other times. Eating more at times may be due to a growth spurt, an increase in activity, or they may not have eaten much the day before.

Here are a few guides on determining the right size portions for your children:

- Children from ages two to eight years need at least two cups of milk or the equivalent each day.

- A good rule of thumb for meat, vegetables and fruit is one tablespoon per year of age for one- to four-year-olds. For example, one serving for a three-year-old child is three tablespoons of a meat, vegetable or fruit.

- Offer smaller portions and then allow them to ask for more. *This can be a key factor in lifetime weight control.*

- Allowing children to eat when hungry and until they are "just satisfied" are good, basic ways to help your children learn the role of food in balancing energy needs.

- Avoid making a child eat everything on his or her plate. Serving smaller portions and allowing the child to ask for more in response to hunger is more appropriate.

- Adding pressure to eat or rewards for eating should not be used. These mechanisms may have a negative impact on long-term food habits and choices.

- Encourage your child to eat more slowly. It helps if the parent sets the example here. Did you know that it takes about 20 minutes before our bodies react to the food we have eaten and send the message to the brain that we are satisfied?

Meal Planning the Heart "E" Heart Way!

One of the most important times each day is mealtime. Unfortunately, many homes today don't have a mealtime. If you don't have one, try to arrange one. Psychologists and family counselors agree that mealtimes with the entire family are critical to a child's sense of family and well-being.

- Make mealtime pleasant! Try to create a warm, friendly atmosphere. Talk and share with one another. Use mealtime to build a positive environment for developing a healthy attitude about food and eating. Use this time to build family relationships. This is not the time to argue or to scold. Building on negative behavior at meals makes mealtime a dreaded time, which can affect your child's eating behavior.

- Successful meals do require some planning. Always include a food that you know your children like. Plan to serve a variety of colors, shapes, tastes and food groups. Visualize how your food will look on a plate. Is it attractive? Alter your menu selections until you can visualize an attractive meal.

- When possible allow your children to help with meal preparation – a great **Heart "E" Heart** learning experience. Involving them in safe tasks such as washing fruit or veg-  etables or stirring a mixture helps to create an interest in foods. Older children can learn to set the table and prepare beverages. And don't forget to ask for help in clearing the table, washing the dishes and putting things away. Sometimes it is a good idea to forget the dishwasher and do the dishes by hand – it gives you more time with your children.

- Including children in daily tasks helps them to be a contributing part of the family unit. As your children are helping you, be sure to talk about how **Heart "E" Heart**  likes to do these kinds of things too! And always recognize their contribution with your appreciation. A hug or a verbal "thank you" will never go unnoticed and this helps to promote positive self-esteem in your child – another good **Heart "E" Heart** experience. But don't use food as a reward for helping prepare or clean-up after a family meal.

- And finally:

  ▸ Family meals eaten at the dining table set the stage for learning positive food behavior. Plan at least one meal per day when the whole family sits down and eats together. Eat meals only in the kitchen or dining areas.

  ▸ Eating together should be fun and a time to build family relationships. Children should not dread mealtime.

  ▸ Avoid distractions at mealtime. Turn off the television and loud music. Return phone calls after meals.

  ▸ Don't rush meals. Most children take more time to eat than adults. Use the extra time for positive conversation.

  ▸ Plan a variety of foods that the whole family will enjoy. New foods or recipes are best accepted if offered with some familiar foods.

  ▸ You should be a good role model for your children. This involves preparing, serving and enjoying eating **Heart "E" Heart** healthy foods on a daily basis. These acts send a positive message to your children that healthy food is good and important for you.

Mealtime also provides the opportunity to teach table manners and social skills such as saying "please" and "thank you," and learning not to interrupt when others are talking. Heart "E" Heart always teaches good manners and respect for each other. Remember, meals with the family are an important part of your children's lives. Make meals a good memory for them.

Don't Use Food to Bribe!

Don't use food to control your children's behavior. Promising a candy bar, cookie or ice cream to behave or to stop crying is wrong. 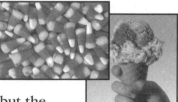 This book is not a book on discipline, but the authors strongly suggest using other approaches to control your children's discipline. Most of the foods used to control a child's behavior are unhealthy – they are Sticky Lipid, Risky Blood Pressure and Bulgy Fat Cell foods. Ice cream and candy can be eaten once in a while but on only special occasions such as birthdays and so on. Exercise and healthy food are the two items that are critical to promoting a healthy lifestyle for your children. These items should not be used in disciplinary actions.

Control Snacking

Coming to the table hungry is a key for your children eating well at meals. Spacing meals and snacks about two to three hours apart is a good idea. Hunger is a natural response to a dip in blood sugar, which occurs when food has not been eaten for awhile. If your children are allowed to eat or drink too close to meals, then their hunger is quenched and they will eat less. When this happens, this is not the time to scold and force your children to eat. Instead, next time do a better job of controlling your children's snacks.

Snacking the Heart "E" Heart Way!

 Because younger children can't eat much at one time, snacks are an important part of their overall nutrition. This is why it is important to provide Heart "E" Heart, Fit Fat Cell and Healthy Blood Pressure healthy snacks such as fresh fruit, raw veggies, various crackers and whole grain cereals. These kinds of snacks help to control your children's hunger between meals. And don't forget to provide your children plenty of low fat milk, water and fruit juices for fluid replenishment.

Children's appetites vary too! So plan to have nutrition-packed foods available to offer as snacks. Because children are growing rapidly and have high nutritional needs, there is not a lot of room for empty-calorie Sticky Lipid, Risky Blood Pressure and Bulgy Fat Cell snacks such as chips, candy, cookies, soda and fruit-flavored beverages. These snacks have a lot of calories but not many vitamins and minerals. When these are the snacks that children eat primarily, their bodies are being packed with sugar and robbed of the building blocks (minerals and vitamins) critical to growth. And don't forget to space meals and snacks about two to three hours apart so snacks do not interfere with meals…this includes milk and juice, too.

Keep a variety of Heart "E" Heart healthy snacks on hand for your children such as the ones listed below.

- ▸ Fresh seasonal fruit
- ▸ Low fat cheese sticks
- ▸ Dry whole grain cereal
- ▸ Natural peanut butter
- ▸ Bite-size raw vegetables, such as carrots or cherry tomatoes
- ▸ Low fat dip for crackers, veggies and fruit
- ▸ Graham crackers
- ▸ Low fat(1 percent) or fat free (skim) milk
- ▸ Low fat yogurt
- ▸ Unsweetened canned fruit

Older Children

School-aged children (six to twelve years) usually do not eat as often as younger children. Keep in mind that their food preferences may change as a result of peer influence at school. Get some input from your children as to foods they like to eat. Guard against having a lot of empty calorie food available – such as chips, cookies, candy and soda – and suggest some healthy Heart "E" Heart alternatives. Children at this age often accept more and more responsibility in their food choices since they are involved more in the preparation. This can be particularly true for children whose parents are working. Often they may prepare breakfast, pack lunch and choose snacks. Parental guidance helps to influence not only their choices now but in later life as well. Identifying Heart "E" Heart foods early in your children's lives will help them make wiser and healthier food choices as they become older.

Choking

Sometimes parents expose their children too early to certain foods they can't chew well. Children who are three and under are at greater risk for choking. Selecting foods to prevent choking is a must. Also, while children at this age are eating, closer supervision is warranted – this is a **Heart "E" Heart** safety recommendation!

Foods that may cause choking are hard foods and foods that are round or in chunks that can get stuck in the throat. Here are some examples:

- Hot dogs
  (Remember **Heart "E" Heart** does not eat these often!)
- Chunks of meat or fruit
- Raw vegetables
- Nuts and seeds
- Raisins
- Grapes
- Cherries
- Popcorn
- Pretzels
- Peanut butter
- Hard candy

Sometimes the solution to prevent choking is simple. For instance,

> ▸ cutting chunks of meat or fruit (for example apples, cherries – watch those seeds, or grapes) into very small pieces

> ▸ cutting hot dogs into small, chewable pieces

> ▸ steaming veggies to soften them

> ▸ spreading peanut butter thin

(Foods such as nuts, seeds, raisins, popcorn, pretzels and hard candy are best left for children ages four and older).

Another area of concern for choking involves the car. When driving with children in the car, never give your children food to eat. Eat in the car only when you can devote complete attention to your children.

Kids and Fat

Due to high energy needs and the need for fat to complete the developing process, it is not a good idea to restrict fat intake for children less than two years of age.

Kids and Fiber

Children need fiber in their daily diet. Normally, foods high in fiber are Heart "E" Heart foods. Scientists agree that fiber plays a role in reducing the risk of heart disease and cancer along with a diet low in saturated fat and cholesterol starting at the early age of two.

In addition, don't forget that fiber helps to create that "just satisfied" feeling by making you feel full. Snack foods high in fiber help to take care of your children's hunger needs between meals. It also prevents constipation. The American Health Foundation uses a simple rule to determine the amount of fiber in grams that a child over the age of three years needs each day.

  ▸ Add five to your child's age. For example, if your child is five years old, add five, which equals ten grams of fiber. This is about one-third of the amount recommended for an adult. The formula accounts for the increasing fiber needs as a child grows older.

  ▸ When following the MyPyramid guidelines, limit juice to less than half of the fruit allowance, eat the recommended level of vegetables and choose one-half of the grams as whole grain for their appropriate calorie level. If young children have difficulty eating this amount of fiber, then *gradually* increase the fiber they are eating.

However, do remember when increasing your children's fiber content to make sure they drink extra fluids, particularly water. Check out Chapter 6 for more fiber facts and the fiber content of specific foods.

Simple, Quick, Nutritious Heart "E" Heart Meals

Don't leave your eating or food preparation to chance. Try to keep some **Heart "E" Heart** foods in the house to work with. Here are some ideas for the various meals during the day to keep your children eating healthy without spending the day in the kitchen. Go easy on the sugar, mayonnaise and margarine. Try the trans free, fat free, light or reduced fat versions of mayonnaise, margarine and salad dressings to cut calories and Sticky Lipids.

Breakfast

A good way to start the day is with breakfast. Try to include some foods with fiber such as a whole grain bread, cereal, or fresh fruit, a low fat dairy product and/or a lean meat or meat substitute. These foods will favor a lower Glycemic Index and promote a more satisfied feeling of fullness.

Try These Heart "E" Heart Breakfast Ideas.

1. Toasted whole grain bagel spread with your choice of natural peanut butter or fat free flavored cream cheese served with fresh banana or your favorite seasonal fruit and skim milk.

2. Plain or toasted lean ham or turkey sandwich spread lightly with mayonnaise accompanied by fresh apple slices or wedges and skim milk.

3. Hot oatmeal or your favorite quick cooking or old-fashioned hot cereal (not instant) served plain or sprinkled with raisins or dried fruit and/or trans free margarine.

Round out your breakfast with cold skim milk and toasted whole grain bread with a dab of jam.

4. Your favorite whole grain cereal with fresh strawberries or your favorite seasonal chopped fruit served with skim milk.

5. Your favorite low fat yogurt topped with dry, crunchy whole grain cereal, fresh chopped berries and nuts along with iced or bottled water.

6. Scrambled egg substitute or egg* sandwich served on toasted or plain whole grain bread with red grapefruit juice or your favorite unsweetened juice.

7. Low fat cheese sticks and whole grain crackers served with your favorite unsweetened, boxed or canned juice.

Remember, egg yolks are high in cholesterol. Avoid eating these daily or plan carefully to eliminate other high cholesterol foods for the day.

Other Quick Heart "E" Heart Healthy Meal Ideas

1. Grilled chicken breast or fish served on a whole grain bun with fresh, sliced tomatoes and crisp spinach leaves topped with honey mustard sauce.

2. Whole wheat tortilla stuffed with black beans, rice and sautéed onions with a sprinkle of sharp cheddar cheese and a splash of salsa. Jalapeño peppers can be added for extra kick.

3. Spaghetti made with "healthy-brand"** sauce, ground round and extra, added mushrooms on a bed of vegetable or whole grain pasta.

**Read food label to make the best decision as to calories, fat and sodium. Try different healthy brands until you find one your family likes.

4. Grilled or baked pork chop, trimmed of fat and served with a baked sweet potato and steamed broccoli, cabbage or your favorite grilled, foil-packed, vegetable combination drizzled with trans free margarine.

5. Roasted or baked chicken sprinkled with your favorite no-salt seasoning served with a baked potato or corn on the cob and steamed, fresh asparagus, green beans, snap peas or boiled greens.

6. Homemade or "healthy-brand" vegetable soup served with your sandwich choice of low fat cheese, lean turkey or natural peanut butter on toasted whole grain bread.

7. "Healthy-brand" hot dog on whole grain bun served with fresh, crunchy baby carrots, cauliflower and broccoli with low fat ranch dressing for dipping.

Round out your **Heart "E" Heart** healthy meals with these suggestions:

Whole grain bread
Fresh green salad
Your favorite vegetable,
    steamed or raw
Fresh, seasonal fruit
Low fat or skim milk
Low fat yogurt

Recipe Substitutions

Don't underestimate the calorie savings from recipe substitutions. When looking at a recipe, always try to improve it by making it healthier. Take a look at the list of common ingredients used in baking and cooking. Is there a healthier substitution you can make? Try the substitution – it will make a difference in calorie count, fat and sugar intake.

> Using **Heart "E" Heart** recipe substitutions can make your special dish healthier. Don't be afraid to try it. You'll be pleased with yourself and the results for taking a step in a healthier direction.

Ingredient	Heart "E" Heart Substitute
Beef, ground	Ground round beef Lean ground turkey Ground venison Reduce the amount by 1/2
Butter	Trans free margarine Margarine (first word on the ingredients listed should be "liquid") *Note:* Reduced fat margarine contains water and can affect the quality of the food prepared unless specifically designed for reduced fat margarine.

Buttermilk	Low fat buttermilk 1 cup fat free (skim) milk + 1 t. vinegar
Cheese	Fat free or low fat cheese Reduce the amount of regular cheese Cheese with 5 grams of fat or less per ounce
Chocolate	1 oz. baking chocolate = 3 TB cocoa or carob powder + 1 TB oil
Cream	Fat free (skim) evaporated milk
Cream cheese	Fat free or light cream cheese (Fat free cream cheese can make cake frosting runny; use less cream cheese or add extra confectioners sugar to get desired consistency.)
Egg, one whole	Two egg whites 1/4 cup cholesterol free egg substitute
Mayonnaise	Fat free or low fat mayonnaise Reduce the amount of regular mayonnaise
Milk, regular or whole	Fat free (skim) or low fat (1 %) milk Reconstituted nonfat dry milk

Nuts	Reduce by 1/2 and toast to nut flavor Dried, chopped fruits
Oil	Canola, olive, soybean, peanut, sesame, corn or safflower oil For sautéing: use fat free broth
Shortening	Trans free shortening Trans free margarine Margarine (first word on label should be "liquid") For quick breads: use oil (see list above) and combine with other liquid ingredients
Sour cream	Fat free sour cream Plain yogurt 1 cup low fat cottage cheese blended with 1-2 t. lemon juice until smooth
Sweetened condensed milk	Fat free sweetened condensed milk
Whipped cream	Fat free nondairy topping Whip chilled evaporated fat free (skim) milk

Chapter 14:
Heart "E" Heart Game Plan
Month by Month for the Entire Year

January

Heart "E" Heart says, "Keep Those New Year's Resolutions Simple."

Happy New Year! Did your family make any New Year's resolutions this year? It's a great time to set some new goals for the year. Setting small, attainable goals toward a larger goal may help in becoming more successful. This is particularly true when it comes to changing lifestyle habits. Keep the goals small and simple!

Here are a couple of suggestions pertaining to diet. Before getting started, take a good look at your family's daily diet. Start keeping track of what your family is eating for three to seven days. Write down everything...when, where and how much was eaten – especially remember those "little" snacks like candy and cookies. Read labels and learn about the caloric content of the foods you are eating. (Remember, the nutrition information is based on the serving size given on the label.) If possible, jot down the caloric content of the foods eaten. Total the calories for the day. Compare your food choices to the recommendations for your calorie level set by MyPyramid (See pages 124-125 or log on to www.mypyramid.gov). Now ask yourself a few questions about your diet.

- Too few vegetables?
- Not enough water?
- Eating fast food too often?
- Indulging in the dessert at dinner too often?
- Too many soft drinks and chips?
- Too many cookies or candy as snacks?
- How can you take some simple steps to improve your diet?

What are you willing to change? Decide on a strategy by changing one to two habits and stick with it for a month. Then re-evaluate after a month to decide if the diet changes have made a difference. For example, eliminating just one 12-ounce soft drink a day means you consume about 140 calories less per day. Replace that soft drink with a glass of water. Just think of what it means to consume 140 calories less per day for a whole year. That is 51,100 calories, which converts into about a 14-pound weight loss.

 How's your family's activity level? Are you getting any exercise? Again, plan to make a change. Decide what your family can do to become more active. It could be that the whole family does some sort of physical activity during TV commercials on Monday, Wednesday and Friday. One suggestion is to stand up and walk in place or do a series of jumping jacks, dancing movements or just walking around the house (without stopping at the refrigera-

tor). In addition, have at least one family weekend outing that is active such as biking, hiking, walking or making a snowman. "The more the merrier" is the **Heart "E" Heart** theme for family exercise and planning a variety of activities will keep everyone interested and moving. Just by adding a little more physical activity (20 minutes – just 10 TV commercials) every day means that you could expend at least 75 calories (adults) more a day than what you currently are doing. Seventy-five calories a day for an entire year means that you will expend 27,375 additional calories, which converts to about an eight-pound weight loss.

By just making two very <u>simple</u> lifestyle changes, eliminating one soft drink a day from your diet and adding just a little bit of physical activity every day, for a whole year, the net result is about a 20-pound weight loss. As a bonus, you actually made three lifestyle changes in that you added a glass of water each day to your diet!

Obviously the increase in physical activity is beneficial to everyone – children and adults. Reducing your calories is necessary if you are overweight. If you are not overweight, it still will do you good to make sure your dietary habits are healthy ones.

Heart "E" Heart always suggests making lifestyle changes that occur slowly – these tend to result in permanent changes. As your family gradually improves its quality of life by eating healthier and getting more exercise, muscles gradually become stronger and overall health improves. And another great benefit is that everyone will feel better and have more energy! Don't forget, if there is a concern for any family member regarding his/her health such as a history of heart disease, check with your doctor before starting an exercise program.

February

Heart "E" Heart says, "It Is Time to Get Moving."

February is Heart Health month and that makes it a special month for **Heart "E" Heart**. So what do you say, do something healthy for your heart. During January, we encouraged you to make one or two small positive lifestyle changes with the beginning of the New Year – **Heart "E" Heart** hopes you have done that and that you are keeping up with those changes.

However, let's make sure you do something this month to strengthen your heart. After all, your heart is a muscle and it too needs exercise to continue to keep it strong or to make it stronger. This makes it easier for the heart to pump oxygen and other nutrients, not only to the heart but to the rest of the body as well. A strong and healthy heart will make you feel better and will help provide you with the energy to get things done. You will be able to feel the difference.

 Aerobic activities help to strengthen the heart. These are activities in which the heart pumps oxygen packed blood to the major muscle groups in areas such as the arms and legs. With the right

kind of exercise, the heart can become stronger. When the heart becomes stronger, it can pump the same amount of blood throughout the body with fewer beats per minute. It truly becomes a fine tuned machine!

How does the heart become a fine tuned machine? An adult heart normally beats about 75 times every minute. A heart that becomes stronger because of exercise might beat only 65 times a minute – but it does the same amount of work.

So how does that protect your heart? Over time it saves thousands of beats, which saves considerable wear and tear on the heart muscle. If you save 10 beats a minute, you are saving 600 beats each hour and that works out to a savings of 14,400 beats each day. Wow and that is only one day. For the whole year, the heart beats 5,256,000 fewer beats – quite a savings in terms of wear and tear on the heart in just one year. Imagine if you did this for ten years! Your savings would be into the tens of millions of beats saved.

Other benefits of aerobic exercise include raising the **Tidy Lipids** (high density lipoproteins that help clear out cholesterol), burning and lowering **Thundering Triglycerides** (stored body fat), and decreasing **Sticky Lipids** (low density lipoproteins that aid in clogging arteries with cholesterol).

So start this month by doing something good for your heart. Here's how:

- Check with your doctor to make sure it's OK to start an aerobic exercise program.

- Choose an exercise that you enjoy and that fits your schedule.

  - Consider walking, biking, jogging, swimming, dancing, stair climbing, skating, exercise classes and/or video exercise tapes.
  - Do activities the whole family will enjoy and choose a combination of indoor and outdoor activities.

- Take five to ten minutes at the beginning of your exercise program to warm-up and at the end take another ten minutes to cool-down. When you do your stretching, make sure your movements are slow and sustained. No bouncing! This will help prevent sore muscles.

- During the exercise session, step up the pace a bit until you produce a light sweat, but are still able to talk or sing without being out of breath. If you can't do this, you are pushing too hard, so slow down a bit.

Start out slowly and gradually increase the time spent in exercise. Try to exercise at least 2-3 times a week for about 15-20 minutes and then over the next few weeks, as you become more fit, increase the aerobic exercise to 4-5 times a week for at least 25-30 minutes. And don't forget the warm-up and cool-down, which is added time to your workout!

Taking time for your heart, after all, is the best valentine you can give to your family and to the special people you love, including yourself! Don't just think about doing it – it is time to do it!

Have a Heart "E" Heart Healthy Month!

Heart "E" Heart says, "Avoid Eating Trans Fatty Acids."

If you have been listening to the news lately, it's likely that you have heard about trans fatty acids. But what are they? Basically, it's oil like soybean or corn oil that has undergone a process called "hydrogenation."

Hydrogenation makes the oil harden. It actually changes the chemical structure of the oil. As a result, the hydrogenated fat does not become rancid as quickly, allowing the food with hydro-genated fat to have a longer shelf life. This means the food will last longer without going bad. It is the hydrogenation process that allows butter or margarine to be formed into a "stick" or for peanut butter to be a spread instead of a liquid.

That may be a good food benefit, but the health effects of hydrogenated fat are not good. In fact, **Heart "E" Heart** says they are absolutely terrible! Besides acting like a saturated fat, which raises our **Sticky Lipids** (low density lipoproteins or "bad cholesterol), it also decreases our **Tidy Lipids** (high density  lipoproteins or "good cholesterol). This presents double trouble for our arteries. The arteries have more **Sticky Lipids** to clog them and fewer **Tidy Lipids** to whisk away the Sticky Lipids – a worst-case scenario in terms of your health!

When reading the ingredient list on a food label, the terms to look for are "hydrogenated" or "partially hydrogenated." Check out the foods you are eating by reading the ingredient list. You may be surprised to find these terms on just about every processed food that you eat –

- microwave popcorn, crackers, cakes, doughnuts, cookies, chips, bread, muffins, pastries, pies, breaded chicken or fish and peanut butter.

And if the list includes shortening or margarine, then that is another trans fat food source. If you eat out, the list goes on. Most restaurants, including fast food restaurants, use hydrogenated-type oil in food preparation, including frying. In fact, the only natural source of trans fat is found in dairy and beef fat, and the levels are low. And **Heart "E" Heart** limits the consumption of these foods anyway!

> **Read the ingredient list and aim for low fat foods and foods that use oil (not palm or coconut oil) instead of hydrogenated or partially hydrogenated fat. This will keep you away from those Sticky Lipid foods.**

Check out foods that have opted not to use hydrogenated fat. A good example is peanut butter – the natural peanut butter, that is – it's "just peanuts"!

Check out these **Heart "E" Heart** tips on how to reduce the amount of trans fat in your diet:

- When eating out, choose foods that are steamed, broiled or grilled instead of fried.

- And if you must have dessert, choose something light, such as sorbet or low fat frozen yogurt with a fresh fruit topping, instead of a baked dessert such as pie, cake or pastry.

- You can also question restaurants about the type of oil they use. Don't simply settle for the response of "vegetable oil" but ask if it contains hydrogenated or partially hydrogenated fat.

- When shopping, choose a trans free margarine or one that lists "liquid oil," such as liquid olive oil, liquid canola oil or liquid corn oil, as the first ingredient on the food label. (Remember, when reading an ingredient list, ingredients are listed in descending order. So the first ingredient is in the highest quantity in the product.)

  - Experts still recommend this type of margarine instead of butter.

- Be sure to read the food label. Labeling laws now require companies to list the amount of trans fat.

- In addition, some trans fat-free foods are being developed. So watch for these new products at the grocery. Even though reading labels is a time-consuming process at first, you will soon learn which are the healthy or Heart "E" Heart products to buy.

- When cooking at home, use oil instead of shortening or margarine when possible.

    • Heart "E" Heart highly recommends olive or canola oil. For example, if you are making a quick bread or muffins and the recipe calls for shortening, substitute the shortening with an equal or slightly less amount of oil and add it to the mixture with the liquid ingredients.

- Pop popcorn the old-fashioned way in which you add the oil to the popcorn or try air-popped popcorn to eliminate the extra fat and calories. Remember, most microwave popcorns contain trans fats or Sticky Lipids.

- Do remember as more and more trans free foods appear on the market, these foods do have calories. The type of fat has been changed. Trans free does not mean calorie free. Do read the food label carefully.

Avoiding trans fatty acids could be one of the best things *you* can do for your health. By eliminating trans fats from your diet, you are limiting Sticky Lipids and many extra calories. Because of this, many people are able to shave away a few extra pounds just by avoiding foods that contain trans fats.

Here is a Heart "E" Heart tip:

> Set a Heart "E" Heart goal for one month. Eliminate trans fats from your diet and your family's diet. Your entire family will benefit from this goal and you will find that it will be easy to continue after one month is over. Oh, and by the way, Heart "E" Heart suggests that you add a daily 15-minute family physical activity period. A real winning combination – less trans fats and more physical activity!

April

Step...Step...Step 1, 2, 3 into Spring and into a Heart "E" Heart

Spring is a great time to increase your physical activity. With warm weather approaching, you'll do almost anything to get outside and enjoy it. So, do take advantage of it by increasing your steps. Yes, that is right, your steps – the number of steps you take each day.

Pedometers have become very popular. These are devices used to measure the number of steps you take. Most of them today are electronic and run off an "AA" battery and can be purchased for as little as $25. Some are a bit more sophisticated and can give you valuable feedback in terms of calories expended, metabolic activity and so on. But the more sophisticated ones cost much more money. Pedometers are small (about the size of a pager) and clip onto your belt. Pedometers can be purchased at most sporting goods stores.

Many people are using pedometers to monitor their daily steps. This is a great way to give you feedback on how you're doing with your walking program. If you have not used a pedometer but always wanted to, now is the time to purchase one. Here are some guidelines to get started:

- Write down, each day for a whole week, how many steps you take in daily activities. Total the daily steps and divide this by seven to give you an average. This is your baseline daily activity.

- Then increase your walking or stepping by taking at least one 30-minute walk, each day, for four or more days each week. Keep a record of your steps.

- Compare your baseline activity to the increased activity week and then set a goal for the number of steps you think you can obtain each day and go for it!

- It is amazing what an additional 30 minutes of walking each day can do for you over a period of one year.

To give you an idea of the number of steps taken per day for different populations, check out the table below:

Population Group	Number of Steps
American children	10,000 – 14,000
Sedentary adults	2,000 – 7,000
Healthy adults	7,000 – 13,000
Healthy older adults	6,000 – 8,500

Heart "E" Heart says any increase in steps helps to improve your physical fitness and burn extra calories. Though some say everyone should walk 10,000 steps per day as an ideal goal, most of the scientific evidence finds that 30 minutes of brisk walking each day is the best overall goal for improving physical fitness and your health. This does not necessarily need to be achieved with one 30-minute continuous walk, but instead can be achieved by taking three 10-minute walks or two 15-minute walks during the day to be effective.

Setting a minimum number of steps per day helps you improve your stepping on those days in which you may be particularly inactive. For instance, when you are riding in the car or sitting at the desk most of the day and your minimum goal is 7,000 steps, then look for creative ways to take those steps. You may walk in place at the copier, take a 10-minute walk at a rest stop if you are driving, or spend your 15-minute break at work by walking outside/inside. And, don't forget opportunities such as taking the stairs and parking the car away from the building! Using your pedometer each day gives feedback on how these little things add to your daily step count.

An unexpected advantage of using your pedometer comes when you can share your experiences with others. Most people who have not used one are curious about it, and those who do use one love to talk about it. And if all it takes is a little pedometer to get you moving more, **Heart "E" Heart** says, "Get one now!"

Heart "E" Heart says, "Eat Lots of Fruits, Vegetables and Grains to Get Your Phytochemicals!"

Phyto who? What on earth are phytochemicals? Don't tell me we need to be concerned about another dietary food! No. Phytochemical is the technical term for antioxidant.

Certainly you have heard vitamin commercials that talk about getting your lutein, lycopene or beta carotene, right? These commercials try to convince you that you are not getting enough of these phytochemicals in your daily diet. Phytochemicals help protect the body against free radicals. Against what? Our bodies produce free radicals daily when we come in contact with things like cigarette or tobacco smoke, radiation from the sun, infections, pesticides, alcohol, carcinogens and physical trauma. Free radicals are unstable and can react with other substances in your body to produce harmful reactions. Until they are neutralized, free radicals continue to multiply and do damage to the cells in our bodies. Tissue damage caused by free radicals promotes the aging process, decreases the effectiveness of our immune system and contributes to chronic diseases such as heart disease, cancer, diabetes and arthritis. Phytochemicals help to neutralize free radicals and protect the body by reducing the risk of these diseases.

There are literally thousands of phytochemicals. The two main classes of phytochemicals are flavonoids and isoprenoids. Here are some examples of these two classes:

Flavonoids	Isoprenoids
flavones	Carotenoids (alpha & beta carotene, lycopene, lutein, beta cryptoxanthin, zeaxanthine)
flavonols	tocopherols
flavanones	tocotrienols
catechins	
antocyanidins	
isoflavonoids	

Do you recognize any of these? There are many more than those listed.

So, do supplements really help? Taking supplements specific to certain phyotchemicals may cause problems. Some research indicates that supplements of beta carotene may actually increase lung cancers in smokers. Remember, there are thousands of phytochemicals found in plants and supplements don't account for all of them. There is much to learn about phytochemicals. But, one thing is clear. Food sources of phytochemicals are very beneficial! And it is **Heart "E" Heart's** recommendation to rely on food sources for your phytochemicals, instead of supplements.

What are the best food sources for phytochemicals? Any food derived from plants. Fruits, vegetables and whole grains are the best food sources! Multiple studies have shown decreased risk of many cancers, heart disease and blood pressure with a high intake of fruits, vegetables and whole grains.

 This is a good time to jump on the phytochemical bandwagon! As the colors of spring emerge… red, yellow, green, orange, purple and blue, think about the plant foods you can eat that match those colors! Healthy, nutritional choices include tomatoes, apples, strawberries, bananas, squash, spinach, yams, grapes and blueberries! The list is endless! Here are a few tips to make sure you include all those colors and plant foods in your daily diet:

- Pack a piece of seasonal fruit for lunch and an afternoon snack.

- Keep fresh, crunchy vegetables, such as baby carrots, cherry tomatoes, cucumbers and celery sticks, ready-to-eat in the refrigerator.

- Include fresh mushrooms, spinach and tomato slices in your sandwich.

- Each day include a variety of whole grains such as brown rice, whole rye bread and whole wheat cereal.

- Plan at least two different vegetables for lunch and dinner; try combining vegetables when cooking to add variety. Try combining potatoes, onions and carrots, broccoli and cauliflower, okra and tomatoes.

- Include plant seasonings, such as basil, parsley and dill, in cooking.

- Experiment with a new recipe that includes tofu, soybeans, or soy flour.

- When making soups or salads, include a variety of vegetables and try some unfamiliar ones occasionally.

Heart "E" Heart recommends that you eat fruits, vegetables and grains, especially whole grains, each day.

June

Start Your Day the Heart "E" Heart Way...with Breakfast!

Starting your day with a healthy, Heart "E" Heart breakfast could be one of the most important new healthy lifestyle habits you try. More and more research is showing why breakfast is important for good health. Let's look at a few reasons.

- Better brain power
- Improved metabolism
- An increase in the day's supply of nutrients
- Reduced risk of obesity, diabetes and heart disease

Now who can resist these benefits?

Better brain power

After fasting overnight, the body craves fuel upon awakening. The brain needs fuel to function well. During the school day, children who eat breakfast perform better on academic tests and can think better, more quickly and more accurately than children who don't. The research also shows that breakfast eaters have better school attendance and are less likely to be depressed.

Improved metabolism

While sleeping, the body's metabolism slows down. Eating breakfast helps to break this cycle and revs up your metabolism, which burns more calories. This conditions the body to calorie-burn the rest of the day. This is a great benefit for those who want to lose weight. In fact, by eating breakfast you are less likely to overeat at other meals and crave high sugar, high fat foods less. Breakfast eaters tend to have a greater chance of losing weight and, more importantly, once the weight is lost, to keep it off.

An increase in the day's supply of nutrients

A well-planned breakfast provides a good portion of the day's nutrients. Heart "E" Heart foods like fat free (skim) milk, fruits and whole grains make for a nutritious breakfast. Remember, there are certain vitamins and minerals that you need each day for the body to function properly. Breakfast should be a meal that is rich in nutrients. Skipping breakfast or eating empty calorie foods for breakfast like donuts, pastries and soda, denies your body the opportunity to start the day right. One advantage of a nutritional breakfast that includes high fiber foods, such as fresh fruit, whole grain breads and cereals, is that feeling of being full. This makes mid-morning snacking on doughnuts and pastries less tempting.

Reduced risk of obesity, diabetes and heart disease

Breakfast skippers have been found to have greater insulin resistance than breakfast eaters. This condition has been strongly associated with obesity, diabetes and heart disease. A Heart "E" Heart breakfast helps to maintain a more steady blood sugar level. This helps you feel better, perform tasks more efficiently and decrease cravings for sweets.

So how can you resist? Not enough time to get breakfast in the morning? You can always prepare the night before by:

- getting clothes ready for the next day
- packing the backpack
- preparing lunches
- if necessary, even selecting a take-along breakfast

How about setting the alarm for a few minutes earlier? Breakfast could be the one meal the family eats together – a good way to start the day.

If you find that you simply can't take the time to stop and eat before school or work, keep some handy items stocked at home that you can grab on the way out the door.

Some examples would be:

- Dry whole grain cereal, individually boxed
- Single serving 100 percent fruit juice
- Apples, bananas, grapes, strawberries, blueberries
- Low fat yogurt
- Homemade cereal mix – pack a variety of whole grain cereal, nuts and dried fruit in a plastic bag
- Whole grain crackers and low fat cheese sticks

So what will it be? Start the day the Heart "E" Heart way to take advantage of all those benefits from a nutritional breakfast, or continue down the path of no breakfast or an empty calorie breakfast? For my family, it is going to be a Heart "E" Heart breakfast!

July

Biking...Great Fun but Be Safe the Heart "E" Heart Way

Biking can be a great way for the whole family to have fun at home and on vacation. There are many bike trails available to let the whole family explore and be active. Whether you are renting bikes on vacation or just getting ready for the summer season, put safety first! An accident that could have been prevented shouldn't spoil the fun.

Here are some Heart "E" Heart safety tips:

1. Make sure the bike fits. When straddling the crossbar with both feet flat on the ground, there should be two

to six inches between the crossbar on the bike and the crotch of the biker. The seat should be high enough so you can touch the ground with the balls of the feet. If the seat is too low, too much pressure is placed on the knee joint. Children should be able to put both feet on the ground when stopping. And the cyclist should be able to comfortably reach the handlebars when sitting on the seat.

2.   Always wear a helmet that has been prop-
erly fitted. The helmet should not twist
or turn. Straps should fit snugly around
the chin. Don't think it looks too cool
to wear a helmet? Well, it's your head
and brain that you are protecting!
That's important! So, purchase
one in your favorite color...a bright
shade is best to help traffic see
you better. If you are transporting
a child, the child needs a bike helmet too!

How old is your helmet? Remember that the helmet becomes more brittle each year no matter how little or how much you use it. If it is more than three years old, you might want to consider purchasing a new one.

3.   Obey all traffic laws as if you were in an automobile. That includes hand signals for turning, stopping at stop signs, riding in the direction of traffic, and if you are riding in a group, ride single file. Don't ride against traffic.

4. Stop, look and listen before crossing roads and streets. Watch out for cars backing out of or turning into driveways. Watch for pedestrians, children playing and other vehicles. It's best to walk your bike across busy intersections using the crosswalks.

5. Choose a safe location to ride. Map out several course options. Perhaps your neighborhood or a bike trail would make for an interesting bike ride. If possible, select a bike trail that is well maintained. Avoid secluded areas, gravel roads, bike trails with large holes and crevices, parking lots and busy roads. Remember, freeways and the interstate roads are off-limits!

6. Make sure you have the appropriate safety gear on your bike. A mirror and horn or bell are a good beginning. A mirror comes in handy, especially if you are riding on the road. Unfortunately, drivers have too many distractions (cell phone, text messaging, CD player, DVD player) when driving their cars, which could be a hazard to you. So keep an eye on the traffic behind you. A bell or horn is helpful when approaching a walker or another cyclist on the bike path to let them know you are passing them. Always pass on the left, and if you don't have a horn, speak up and say, "on your left." Another safety item is a cell phone. Bring your cell phone with you to use should an emergency occur, but riding and talking on the cell phone is not a good idea.

7. Clowning around is not wise when biking. Keep both feet on the pedals. Keep both hands on the handlebars

except when signaling. And, no extra passengers riding on the handlebars.

8. Leave the headphones at home. Listening to music while riding prevents you from hearing critical sounds that are important to your safety, such as approaching vehicles and horns from cars or other cyclists. You also miss the sounds of mother nature, such as chirping birds, when on a bike trail.

9. Wear the right gear, such as shoes that grip the pedals, slim pants that won't get hung in the chains, light clothing so you can be seen and shatterproof sunglasses. A fanny pack with sunscreen, insect spray and a water bottle are musts for summer months.

10. And, don't forget to do a quick check to make sure your bike is in safe working order before starting your journey. Wheels, gears, pedals, chains, seat, handlebars and frame should be well maintained and checked periodically.

    • Check the tire pressure. It is not uncommon for a bike tire to lose some air pressure over time. Keeping the tires at the correct pressure is important to ensure a smooth and efficient ride. Be sure to check the tire pressure with a pressure gauge – don't guess! A tire pressure gauge can be purchased for a couple of dollars and the correct pressure can be found on the side of the tire.

    • For a nominal fee, a local bike shop can perform a maintenance check on your bike each year.

And away you go! What a great adventure each time you climb on your bike. And remember parents, teaching bike safety and setting a good example for your children can make these adventures even more fun and reduce the possibility of injuries.

August

Heart "E" Heart says, "Prepare the Right Way for Labor Day."

Labor Day is just around the corner - our last hurrah of the summer! Heart "E" Heart wants you to remember to make it a healthy and active weekend!

The weather can still be pretty warm - so plan some outdoor activities while you still have the chance. Check out your local trails for some biking and/or hiking. If you live near a river, canoeing could be an option - but don't forget those lifejackets. Swimming is always popular - and good for you too! But remember to never swim alone or dive into an unfamiliar area.

August is a good month to continue with visits to the local farmers' market - especially if you are in the Midwest. Most fruits and vegetables, grown locally, are now at their peak. Sweet corn is especially delicious now. Fruits and vegetables are a great way to fill up without loading up on calories but avoid adding the extra butter and salt.

Now is also a good time to plan for the winter months. Many fruits and vegetables freeze well. Choose your favorites and start stocking up for freezing. It is a great way to have the fresh fruits and vegetables of the summer in January!

August is also the time for pre-season training for students and professionals involved in fall sports. Very often this training takes place outdoors. It is essential that you stay hydrated – drink water frequently. Don't wait until you are thirsty. Also, avoid caffeinated and sugary drinks as they can contribute to dehydration. And, don't forget the sunblock. Reapply frequently as you begin to perspire.

Heat stroke is a very real danger this time of year. Stop what you are doing if you begin to feel chilled or disoriented and seek medical attention. Find out, before you begin your training, the guidelines for preventing heat stroke from your family physician, team trainer or doctor. Know the symptoms – it could save your life! Remember...Heart  "E" Heart always puts safety first. Remember, heat stroke can occur at any age. Make sure your young children drink plenty of fluids since they are more prone to dehydration.

Have a great and active month of August!

September

Let Heart "E" Heart Help You Get Ready for School.

With school beginning, often the school cafeteria or vending machine provides your children lunch. In most cases, this makes

breakfast even more critical. Too often, breakfast is overlooked. Studies have shown that children who eat breakfast perform better in school. If time is tight, lay out clothing the night before and pack the lunches too. Cereal, fruit, toast and bagels are all quick and nutritious. If that still doesn't fit into your schedule, there are breakfast-to-go alternatives, such as oatmeal and granola bars. Be sure to avoid the bars with candy and extra sugar added to them.

We don't want to ignore lunches either. It is better to send your children to school with a lunch instead of relying on cafeteria food or vending machines. By packing their lunch, you still have some influence on your children's nutrition. Shop for items that are easy to pack, such as low fat lunchmeat for sandwiches and fruits and veggies like apples, bananas and baby carrots. Or perhaps you were successful with a summer garden! Harvest the fruits and/or vegetables you planted and enjoy them this fall! Snacks like portable yogurts and small bags of pretzels are also popular. And, if beverages aren't provided, shop for low fat milk cartons or low-sugar juice boxes. Soda and high-sugar juice are fine occasionally, as well as the fast lunch like pizza or burgers.

When students get home, their stomachs are often empty. Keep quick and easy healthy snacks on hand, like fruit and veggies already cut and ready to eat, graham crackers and milk or water to drink. But don't forget to maintain physical activity! Head outside for some games like tag, soccer, or climbing on the jungle gym. If weather is not permitting, try the local YMCA or community center for open gyms or planned activity. It is important to maintain regular activity during the school year too, as studies have also shown that students who are physically active perform better in school than their inactive counterparts.

Heart "E" Heart wants all of his friends to study hard and have a great and healthy September!

October

October! Doesn't Matter Where You Are...What a Great Month!

Fall colors are in bloom. For some individuals, it is really the last month to get out and enjoy beautiful - usually mild - weather. Check out your local and state parks for some biking and hiking. As always, don't forget the safety gear - even if you are hiking. Depending upon the terrain, helmets and elbow and knee pads might be in order.

And, of course, October is the big candy month - it's Halloween. Remember safety when choosing your costumes as well as devising a trick-or-treat plan. Choose your route ahead of time - make sure it is well lit. Be sure the children do not consume any candy before returning home. You can then inspect the bag with proper lighting. It is a good idea to limit your trick-or-treating to familiar homes or an organized event - like at your local zoo.

October is an exciting month. It is a transition month, between summer and winter and change is constant. Enjoy it in a Heart "E" Heart way and you're sure to have fun!

November

Heart "E" Heart says, "Start Preparing for the Holidays Early."

In November we are moving into the holiday time of year. Many of you are making plans for family gatherings or special vacations. There are so many things to do! Often we tend to neglect our eating and exercise habits and, as a result, when we finally do manage to get on the scales in January, there are a few extra pounds. This year can be different, but it does take a plan and strategy.

Here are a few Heart "E" Heart menu planning suggestions.

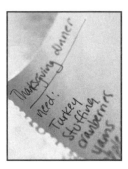

- Every family has its favorite holiday foods. Try substituting some fat free items, such as fat free sour cream, fat free cream cheese or evaporated skim milk, into your recipes.

- Or, try reducing the amount of margarine or mayonnaise you use. Include in your menu some lower calorie, delicious foods like steamed, fresh broccoli or asparagus, a seasonal fresh fruit salad or tossed spinach salad.

238

- Include some homemade, whole wheat yeast rolls. The smell of fresh baked bread will make your home smell wonderful, inviting and **Heart "E" Heart** healthy!

Here are a few Heart "E" Heart physical activity alternatives.

- Planning a family activity or outing can make this year's holidays both memorable and healthier.

- Try to do something everyone will enjoy. It could be building a snowman, going to the tree farm to tag this year's Christmas tree, walking on the beach or around the neighborhood to look at the outdoor holiday decorations, or simply gathering pecans under the tree in the backyard.

Getting the whole family involved in making this a healthier holiday season will make the plan more successful. The plan could be as simple as eating smaller portions of rich, high calorie foods or taking 20-minute family walks as many days as possible during the holidays, especially on the day of celebration itself (and then hopefully you will continue after the holiday season). However, no matter what **Heart "E" Heart** strategy you take, it's a step in the right direction.

Heart "E" Heart Really Likes the Holidays but Don't Forget Your Diet and Exercise.

December is here and there's plenty to do! Among the hustle and bustle of the holidays, it is easy to neglect our **Heart "E" Heart** habits, particularly healthy eating and exercise.

- This is a good time to concentrate on those healthy daily lifestyle habits, like parking away from stores when shopping and taking the stairs instead of the elevator or escalator. **Heart "E" Heart** is always safe, however and is sure to park near a light if it is late in the day. If you are by yourself, park closer to the door and walk briskly around the mall a few times first. You can window shop and plan your shopping trip while you burn some extra calories. Or, while at home take a quick break from the wrapping and the shopping for a brisk walk around your block... don't forget your hat, coat and gloves though, if the weather is cold. Don't overdress – remember to dress in layers! Take the kids with you and you can enjoy the various snowmen and lights in the neighborhood and then build a snowman in your own yard when you return.

- Keeping some easy to prepare foods around the house also makes it less tempting to eat fast foods when you're out. Many food companies have created a healthier line of canned soups that are high in vegetables and low in sodium. Give those a try to keep you warm and healthy too! Keep plenty of whole grain breads, low fat sandwich meat, raw veggies, baked chips, fresh fruits, low fat milk, yogurt and cheese on hand. This will keep your family's nutrition in check and will free time and money for other things. The better nourished we are before we leave the house, the less likely we are to indulge at the food court or strip malls. Save the indulgences for the holiday meals and treats you prepare for that special day.

Make this holiday a **Heart "E" Heart** gift giving theme. When buying gifts for people, keep in mind Heart "E" Heart items that will help them stay active, fit and healthy. Here are a few ideas:

- bikes, ice skates, rollerblades, pedometers (to track the number of steps you take during the day), and balls (soccer, basketball, football, baseball, tennis and golf)

- gear for any sport, like socks, shoes or sweats, or helmets, gloves, and accessories for a specific activity, like cycling

- children's toys that promote physical activity or movement, instead of toys that promote sitting still such as video games. Tricycles, area rugs with active games like hopscotch woven into the carpet, floor hockey games and climbing toys are all good choices. Make sure the toy fits your child.

- books on healthy cooking, recipes, games, fitness and health—don't forget **Heart "E" Heart's** stories!

These are all gifts that will help that special someone get off to a healthy start in the New Year.

Have a happy and healthy holiday season from **Heart "E" Heart** and friends! Be safe, stay fit, eat right and have fun!

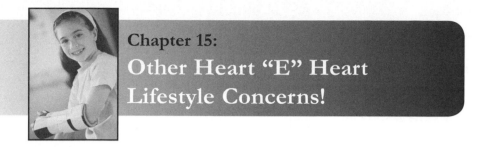
Our final background information chapter deals with other lifestyle issues that are particular to children. Heart "E" Heart presents information on child safety for such topics as poisons, smoking, fire, strangers, personal hygiene and so on. As you read through this chapter, discuss these topics with your child using Heart "E" Heart as the gold standard. *Remember,* Heart "E" Heart *never wants to compromise the safety of your child.*

Safety

Heart "E" Heart not only believes in proper exercise and healthy eating but also in keeping himself safe from harm. Heart "E" Heart has learned valuable safety lessons in the home, school and community. Heart "E" Heart always obeys safety rules and regulations.

▸ At Home, Heart "E" Heart:

  ■ Knows to call 911 if there is a fire or if someone is badly hurt or sick or in need of help.

  ■ Is careful not to play with electrical outlets. (Be sure to cover the outlets with the child protector inserts. These can be purchased at a local hardware store.)

- Doesn't play with matches. (Be sure to keep matches and items related to fire in a secure area – such as locked drawer.)

- Stays away from food to which he is allergic and finds out if any of his friends have food allergies when they visit.

- Knows his neighbors and feels comfortable going to them if he needs help.

- Does not let strangers into his home and does not tell strangers personal information over the phone or Internet.

▶ **At School, Heart "E" Heart:**

- Never accepts rides from strangers on the way to school or on the way home.

- Is careful not to leave sharp objects lying about his desk or on the floor.

- Wears proper attire (including shoes) in gym class and recess and does not wear clothing that is too tight or way too big.

- Gets help from a teacher if another student is bullying him or other children.

- Never brings knives or guns to school – and never plays with them anywhere! If he sees other children with these items, **Heart "E" Heart** will tell his teacher immediately.

▶ In the Community, Heart "E" Heart:

- Knows his neighborhood and knows where not to go without supervision.

- Never talks to or goes near a stranger.

- Is very careful playing at the playground — he doesn't jump off high objects and sits on swings with his feet in front.

- Is careful to look both ways before crossing the street.

- Wears a helmet when he rides a bike and wears the appropriate safety gear when doing other activities such as rollerblading, skateboarding and so on.

- Bikes, skateboards and rollerblades only in designated areas.

▶ In our society, we use many different signs for safety and help. Heart "E" Heart knows these helpful signs:

- **911:** to call for emergencies

- **Block Parent:** a home that children can go to if they need assistance

- The universal sign for **NO**. A circle with a line through it means do not do that activity or that activity is not permitted.

  - Over a swimmer - no swimming allowed.
  - Over a bike - no biking allowed.
  - Over a walker - do not walk.

Can you think of other signs to review with your child?

■ **Exit Sign:** In case of emergency, use a door or window that has "exit" over or below it. (Make sure your child knows the exit sign).

■ **Poison Symbol:** The object or container contains a poisonous substance. Do not drink or eat the substance. Stay away from it. Don't even open it because the fumes may be harmful.

■ **Flammable Symbol:** The container or object is flammable. Keep fire and heat away from these containers or objects.

▶ **Heart "E" Heart** knows what to do about medicines.

  ■ Friends of Heart "E" Heart know and obey the following rules when it comes to medicines/drugs:

    • Never take medicine or drugs from another child

    • Never take medicine or drugs from a stranger

    • Never take medicine out of a medicine chest, cupboard or similar container

    • Take medicines only from:
        a parent or older relative (aunt/uncle etc.)
        a teacher
        a doctor/nurse

    • Always take prescribed medicines as directed

▶ Heart "E" Heart avoids dangerous drugs!

■ There are different kinds of drugs. Some drugs, such as prescribed medicines, are meant to be helpful when taken as directed. Other drugs can cause harm, illness or death.

■ Drugs that can cause immediate harm are:
  • Speed (or something similar)
  • Cocaine
  • Heroin
  • Marijuana
  • Alcohol
  • Ecstasy
  • Similar or related drugs

■ Some drugs are found in food we eat or drink and may cause harm if consumed over time.

  • Caffeine found in soft drinks, coffee, chocolate, and cocoa

  • Nicotine, a drug that is found in tobacco. It can cause harm to the body over time, which is another reason not to smoke.

Smoking – Smoker Heart

Heart "E" Heart wants your child to get to know Smoker Heart. Smoker is weak and purplish looking for a reason. Check out the information on the next page to find out why and discuss with your child.

Tobacco is a plant grown, dried and then made into tobacco products such as cigarettes, pipe tobacco and snuff or chew. Tobacco products contain a powerful drug called nicotine, which causes an increase in blood pressure (**Risky Blood Pressure**), in triglycerides (**Thundering Triglyceride**) and in LDL (**Sticky Lipid**). Here is what else nicotine can do to the body:

- Nicotine constricts the blood vessels and this can reduce the amount of blood pumped by the heart.

- Nicotine causes the heart rate to increase even when a person is at rest.

- Nicotine has been proven to be addictive.

- Smoking produces a toxic substance called *carbon monoxide.*

  - Nicotine and carbon monoxide may cause damage to the walls of the arteries, allowing fatty deposits (**Sticky Lipids**) to form more easily in the walls, which can lead to *hardening of the arteries (atherosclerosis).*

  - In the blood, the carbon monoxide replaces oxygen, which deprives the body and especially the heart of this important substance. With less oxygen, the heart muscle is weakened and becomes purplish in color. (**Smoker Heart**)

- *Second-hand* or *downstream smoke* is also harmful. Some research shows that second-hand smoke may be more harmful for children than smoking itself.

- Long-term smoking and/or tobacco chewing causes damage to the cells in the lungs, throat and mouth, and may lead to cancer in those areas of the body.

- Smokers often substitute smoking for eating, and smoking leaves a bad taste in one's mouth. Because of this, smokers are often nutritionally depleted.

- Other negative aspects of smoking include bad breath, a chronic raspy cough, clothes that smell like stale smoke and yellow teeth.

- Quitting smoking increases HDL. (Tidy Lipid)

Remember to review these safety concerns with your child on an ongoing basis. Sometimes it can be done in conjunction with a specific activity. For example, when going for a bike

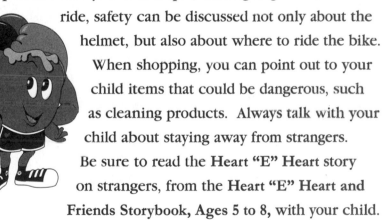

ride, safety can be discussed not only about the helmet, but also about where to ride the bike. When shopping, you can point out to your child items that could be dangerous, such as cleaning products. Always talk with your child about staying away from strangers. Be sure to read the Heart "E" Heart story on strangers, from the Heart "E" Heart and Friends Storybook, Ages 5 to 8, with your child.

To order this storybook or any other books in this series, go to our website: www.moveitloseitlivehealthy.com.

APPENDIX

Appendix A: Daily Physical Activity Log

Exercise Type	Date	Date	Date	Date	Date	Date	Date
Strength	Sets/ Reps/ Wt	Sets/ Reps/ Wt	Sets/ Reps/ Wt	Sets/ Reps/ Wt	Sets/ Reps/ Wt	Sets/ Reps/ Wt	Sets/ Reps/ Wt
Cardiovascular	Time/ Dist	Time/ Dist	Time/ Dist	Time/ Dist	Time/ Dist	Time/ Dist	Time/ Dist

Exercise Type	Date	Date	Date	Date	Date	Date	Date
Stretching							
Sports							
Chores							

Appendix B: Food and Activity Log

Instructions for Completing Food/Activity Log:

1. Choose at least three days that are typical. Include at least one weekend day.

2. Writing down where foods are eaten may help in defining if eating in certain places makes you more vulnerable to eating less than healthy. Examples: car, desk, living room, kitchen

3. Jot down your mood. Terms such as angry, mad, lonely, sad, happy or bored could be used. Moods associated with overeating need to be identified so when they occur, new, learned behavior not associated with eating can be used. For example, rather than overeating when you are angry, taking a walk would be more productive in reducing your waistline.

4. Keeping track of when you eat (time) may give insight into whether or not you are spacing food intake throughout the day or cramming it all in a short time.

5. Write down amounts (how much) in household measures such as cups, ounces, milliliters. This will identify if controlling portion sizes is a problem.

6. Calculate or estimate calories using available information such as food labels or fast food nutrition information. You may decide to purchase a calorie counting book or check out the website for the USDA Nutrient Database (See www.nal.usda.gov/fnic/cgi-bin/nut_search.pl).

7. Be sure to log your physical activity (no matter how little), how long you spent doing the activity and how hard you felt you were working/exercising.

8. Tally the number of foods eaten from each of the food groups and compare to the number recommended by the MyPyramid Food Intake Pattern for your calorie goal or level. In the blank spot under the Recommended Number on the Food Group Tally sheet, complete the number for the food group that is outlined for your calorie level.

Activity Log: Day 1

Describe Activity	How Long (minutes)	Describe Intensity (hard, easy)

Food Group Tally: Day 1

Food Group	Recommended Number	Your Tally	Your Total
Grain Group			
Vegetable Group			
Fruit Group			
Milk, Yogurt, Cheese Group			
Meat, Poultry, Fish, Beans, Eggs, Nuts Group			
Fats and Oils Group			
Discretionary Calories			

Day 1 - Date: _____

Where	Mood	Time	How Much	What	Calories

Activity Log: Day 2

Describe Activity	How Long (minutes)	Describe Intensity (hard, easy)

Food Group Tally: Day 2

Food Group	Recommended Number	Your Tally	Your Total
Grain Group			
Vegetable Group			
Fruit Group			
Milk, Yogurt, Cheese Group			
Meat, Poultry, Fish, Beans, Eggs, Nuts Group			
Fats and Oils Group			
Discretionary Calories			

Day 2 - Date: _____

Where	Mood	Time	How Much	What	Calories

Activity Log: Day 3

Describe Activity	How Long (minutes)	Describe Intensity (hard, easy)

Food Group Tally: Day 3

Food Group	Recommended Number	Your Tally	Your Total
Grain Group			
Vegetable Group			
Fruit Group			
Milk, Yogurt, Cheese Group			
Meat, Poultry, Fish, Beans, Eggs, Nuts Group			
Fats and Oils Group			
Discretionary Calories			

Day 3 - Date: _____

Where	Mood	Time	How Much	What	Calories

Appendix C: www.moveitloseitlivehealthy.com

Please feel free to go to the www.moveitloseitlivehealthy.com website to do the following:

- Download and print the Daily Physical Activity Log
- Download and print the Food and Activity Log

In addition to the above, the website provides links to other healthy lifestyle websites, including a link to a list of foods for the Glycemic Index.

To make sure you keep up with the latest physical activity and nutrition news, a monthly newsletter is available that can be downloaded via the Internet or mailed to your home.

The website provides information on other products and services that might be of interest and are designed to help you achieve and maintain a healthy body weight and physically active lifestyle.

REFERENCES

References

Internet Resources

American Dietetic Association: www.eatright.org

National Institutes of Health: www.nih.gov

What You Need to Know About Mercury in Fish and Shellfish: www.cfsan.fda.gov/~dms/admehg3.html

Guidance on How to Understand and Use the Nutrition Facts Panel on Food Labels: www.cfsan.fda.gov/~dms/foodlab.html

Trans Fat Now Listed With Saturated Fat and Cholesterol on the Nutrition Facts Label: www.cfsan.fda.gov/~dms/transfat.html

Phytochemicals - Vitamins of the future?: http://ohioline.osu.edu/hyg-fact/5000/5050.html

MyPyramid: www.mypyramid.gov

American College of Sports Medicine: www.acsm.org/health%2Bfitness/fit_society.htm

Other References

American Dietetic Association: <u>Position of the American Dietetic Association: Health Implications of Dietary Fiber</u>, J. Am. Diet. Assoc. 2002; 102:993-1000. (Expires 2007)

American Dietetic Association: <u>Position of the American Dietetic Association: Use of Nutritive and Nonnutritive Sweeteners</u>, J. Am. Diet. Assoc. 2004;104:255-275.

Foster-Powell, K., Holt, S. and Brand-Miller, J. C.: <u>International table of glycemic index and glycemic load values</u>: 2002, Am. J. Clin. Nutr. 2002;76:5-56.

Le Masurier, G. C.: <u>Walk Which Way?</u>, ACSM's Health & Fitness Journal. 2004; 8(1):7-10.

Mitchell, M.K. <u>Nutrition Across the Lifespan</u>, Second Edition. Philadelphia, Pennsylvania: W.B. Saunders Co. 2003. 608 pp.

<u>National Cholesterol Education Program Report of the Expert Panel on Blood Cholesterol Levels in Children and Adolescents</u>, Pediatrics. 1992; 89 (Suppl):525-584.

Pennington, Jean A.T. and Douglass, Judith S. <u>Bowes & Church's Food Values of Portions Commonly Used</u>, 18th edition. Baltimore, Maryland: Lippincott Williams and Wilkins. 2004. 452 pp.

Williams, C.L. et al: <u>A new recommendation for dietary fiber in childhood</u>. Pediatrics. 1995; 96:985-988.

INDEX

273

About the Authors

Thomas B. Gilliam, Ph. D. - Dr. Gilliam is a pioneer and acknowledged expert in the field of dynamic strength testing for industry based on the sports medicine model. Dr. Gilliam has provided isokinetic physical capability assessments for Fortune 1000 companies since 1982. Dr. Gilliam's programs have dramatically reduced worker's compensation costs and decreased injury incidence and severity rates for major industrial clients.

In addition, Dr. Gilliam has been instrumental in identifying and presenting to industry the higher risk for injury and disease caused by obesity in the workplace.

Dr. Gilliam is the creator of the Heart "E" Heart program, which is a healthy lifestyle program for children and their families. Dr. Gilliam was the principal investigator in a National Institutes of Health research study investigating the impact of physical activity and nutritional habits on heart disease risk in young children. This research in the late 1970s resulted in numerous scholarly publications and television and radio interviews throughout the world including NBC's *Today Show* and NBC's *Nightly News* with their science editor, Robert Basel.

In 1973, Dr. Gilliam earned a doctorate degree from Michigan State University in exercise physiology with a minor in graduate statistics and research design. From 1974 to 1982, Dr. Gilliam was on the faculty at the University of Michigan. Before resigning from his tenured faculty position, he was involved with numerous funded research projects (i.e. N.I.H., Kellogg Foundation, State of Michigan and others) that resulted in 29 refereed, scholarly publications.

Jane C. Neill, R.D., L.D. - Ms. Neill is the 2004 recipient of the Nutritionist of the Year Award for the State of Alabama Public Health. She is an active member of the American Dietetic Association and currently employed by the Alabama Department of Public Health, where she works with the WIC (Women, Infants and Children) program as a WIC coordinator and a licensed dietitian. Ms. Neill has worked in the WIC program for over ten years, providing daily nutrition counseling for women, infants and children.

While on the staff as a registered dietitian at the University of Michigan Health System in the late 1970s, Ms. Neill was instrumental in working with Dr. Gilliam as an investigator on the National Institutes of Health research study to investigate the impact of physical activity and nutritional habits on heart disease risk in children ages six to eight years.

Ms. Neill was a member of the team that developed and wrote the Heart "E" Heart program for children and their families.

Ms. Neill received her bachelor's of science degree from the University of Alabama in 1977 in food, nutrition and institutional management. Ms. Neill has been working as a registered dietitian for over 27 years.